Merleau-Ponty and a Phenomenology of PTSD

Merleau-Ponty and a Phenomenology of PTSD

Hidden Ghosts of Traumatic Memory

MaryCatherine McDonald

LEXINGTON BOOKS
Lanham • Boulder • New York • London

Published by Lexington Books
An imprint of The Rowman & Littlefield Publishing Group, Inc.
4501 Forbes Boulevard, Suite 200, Lanham, Maryland 20706
www.rowman.com

6 Tinworth Street, London SE11 5AL, United Kingdom

British Library Cataloguing in Publication Information Available

Library of Congress Cataloging-in-Publication Data Is Available

ISBN 978-1-4985-8042-7 (hardback)
ISBN 978-1-4985-8043-4 (electronic)

For Dad, who never forgot the sound of the cockroaches skittering across the floor in Vietnam.

Contents

Acknowledgments

The process of thanking those who have been instrumental in the completion of this book feels almost as daunting as writing it to begin with. We have an illusion about writing: that one simply sits down and writes. Alone. In a well-lit room. Ideally with a grant. And then it's done. This is *far* from true. Writing something like this is a bit like catching an illness. It lives inside of you and though you may be doing other things, it's always there, waiting. This makes thanking those who have been involved especially difficult because if you were being honest, you'd have to include everyone you encountered along the way. There are those who help directly—by reading drafts, talking through ideas, and providing research sources. Then there are those who help indirectly—by being themselves, believing in you, making sure that you eat and sleep and laugh, and remind you of why you started this process in the first place. Finally, there are those who plant seeds and help without knowing it at all. People who ask you questions at conferences that undo or reframe everything, people who you sit next to on planes who ask you what you do, Uber drivers who open up about their personal trauma when you mention what you're working on, strangers who say random things that stick, the people that write and produce the music that keeps you writing when you don't think you have anything left to say, and of course any and all purveyors of caffeine. There are pieces of all of them here.

More specifically (though incompletely): Thank you to the College of the Holy Cross and Old Dominion University for the grant funding that made this research possible. Thank you to my wonderful colleagues and administrators at Holy Cross and Old Dominion for supporting me. Thank you to my friends and family who regularly do more to help than they could possibly know. Thank you to my wonderful editors at Lexington Press. And thank you especially to those of you who have shared your stories with me. It has been an honor.

Prologue

We have been studying the common cold with tenacity since about 1946, when the Medical Research Council set up the Common Cold Unit in the United Kingdom. The impetus for such focus on such an—well, common—ailment was the war. Posters during World War II point out the egregious impact that the cold has on the war effort. The text on one poster reads:

> Work it out like this.
> On an average 2 days work are lost a year by each worker
> Say there are 10 million people on vital war production
> That means 20 million days lost each year—
> The work of 50,000 men for one year.
> IF one third of all the men and women who lost these days were making tanks, one third bombers, and one third rifles
> Then in that time they could make
>
> 3,500 TANKS
> 1,000 BOMBERS
> 1,000,000 RIFLES
>
> That is the cost to our war effort. We can all help to reduce that cost. Do your bit to prevent the spread of infection—by trapping the germs in a handkerchief when you cough or sneeze.
>
> HELP TO KEEP THE NATION FIGHTING FIT.[1]

There are several things worth noticing here. First, it is clear that efficiency is not just a value but a *necessity*. The cold may not be deadly, but a weak country is. Further, this job—keeping the nation fighting fit!—falls on the shoulders of *everyone*, not just the soldier. "We can all help to reduce that cost." Notice also that the value is placed specifically on *physical* fitness. Physical ailments, even the most benign and temporary ones, are worth being protected from.

When it comes to the notion of coming to the aid of those who suffer psychologically, on the other hand, we are not motivated by posters to "do our bit." Combat veterans suffer in silence. Not only in the sense that they suffer without speaking of their trauma, which they sometimes do, but also in the sense that they are *surrounded by silence.* It is not—nor has it ever been—societally acceptable to speak of one's psychological wounds.

Stigma is one of the many reasons that the history of the study of trauma has been maddeningly episodic. Another reason is that, though people may be traumatized by many different kinds of events, sustained scientific study of trauma tends to be concentrated around large-scale disasters. Immediately after wars, earthquakes, devastating hurricanes, or terror attacks, there is an uptick in interest in trauma. However, when peacetime comes, the earth stops shaking, flood-waters recede, and senseless attacks on civilians fade into the past, interest in the study of trauma also fades. We might term this the disaster-model study of trauma.

The disaster-model study of trauma began essentially by accident, and, as is the case with so many of our personal and collective psychological maladies, this can be traced back to (and some would argue blamed on) Freud. It was Sigmund Freud and his colleague Josef Breuer (following in the footsteps of Pierre Janet and Jean-Martin Charcot) who discovered that when events were too overwhelming to bear, they could create a strange tension in the victim: a tension whereby the event would lodge itself in the psyche, begging to be told, all the while defying being told. This tension between wanting to be revealed and concealed simultaneously could result in some strange symptoms in the victim: anxiety, dissociative states, mutism, digestive problems, and so on.

Entirely by chance, Freud and Breuer discovered that if the story could be revealed to the therapist in a safe and trusting environment, the symptoms often faded away completely. They theorized that this was a result of abreaction and catharsis—the release of the emotion tied to the event, and then the purging of those emotions in the presence of a safe and stable therapist. In their words:

> For we found, to our great surprise at first, that *each individual hysterical symptom immediately and permanently disappeared when we had succeeded in bringing clearly to light the memory of the event by which it was provoked and in arousing its accompanying affect, and when the patient had described that even in the greatest possible detail and had put the affect into words.*[2]

It is worth noting the surprise—Freud and Breuer were casting about in the darkness and stumbled upon what we now call "the talking cure." Though there is lasting truth to what they discovered here, they infamously abandoned their work and their patients, many of whom continued to suffer greatly. Once they figured out what was going on—and it is worth mentioning that most of their patients were women who had suffered sexual traumas at the hands of their friends and superiors in society—they packed up their things, left their patients high and dry, and moved on from their work.

So began the long history of the episodic study of trauma. There are several moments in history in which trauma became the focus of humanitarian and scientific study for a specific reason (most notably: World War I, World War II, Vietnam, 9/11) and then gradually that focus waned. This is not to say that there is *no* study of trauma going on in between disasters, just that study becomes less popular, it is seen as less necessary, and thus less likely to get funding.

There are several problems with an episodic study of trauma. Because we keep closing the study, we are forced to reinvent the wheel in some sense each time we open it up again. Each time a disaster happens, we are left scrambling for old remedies while trying to forge forward in the midst of chaos. This is not the most fruitful way to make progress.

Perhaps even more problematically, this disaster-model of trauma study also operates on a false assumption that the only relevant traumas are those that are suffered during wartime, a terror attack, or a natural disaster. Those suffered at the hands of an abusive partner, or because of a traumatic loss or chronic illness, do not seem to count. Not only are we studying it episodically, we are also constructing a hierarchy of traumas in which certain experiences get to "count" as traumatic and others do not. This is destructive for those in both camps, those whose experiences "count" can become fetishized, and those who do not are forgotten.

At the moment, combat trauma is an especially urgent issue. Current reports on veteran suicide data estimate that twenty-two veterans commit suicide every day, and this is a statistic that is cited often. What many people do not know is that these current reports do not include veterans who have been dishonorably discharged, nor those who are active service members, nor those who die by overdose, nor the deaths that occur in Texas and California as these states have not provided data. There is a significant reason, then, to think that the actual number of suicides due to military related post-traumatic stress disorder (PTSD) is much higher than twenty-two people a day.[3]

There have been attempts to figure out just why treating PTSD is so difficult, and each has pointed to a different villain. Some cite our inability to connect emotionally to one another in general. Others blame our contradictory social mores that demand that soldiers remain simultaneously heroically pure while they commit what we normally deem atrocities. It is certainly possible that all of these factors play a role in the prevalence of PTSD. What is perhaps more likely is that we struggle to successfully treat PTSD *because we do not understand it well enough.* The episodic study of trauma, alongside several other factors that I will focus on in this book, has led to a fractured understanding of it, and the only way to fix this is to pick up all of the pieces and attempt to put them back together.

To that end, I have two goals here. The first is to build a prismatic approach to trauma (one that aims to see trauma in three dimensions) by bringing the perspectives of psychology and neuroscience together with phenomenology. I advocate for this prismatic approach because beyond the problem of the disaster-model study of trauma, there is also the fact that the disciplines that study trauma are often siloed from one another. Since each of the sciences have their own history and approach to understanding and treating trauma, they are at best working on the same problem in two different spaces, and at worst they are often thought to be incompatible and pursuing wholly different goals.

Further, they have been missing the philosophical voice, which is critical to understanding trauma. This brings me to the second goal of the book, which is to bring the perspective of phenomenology into the conversation. Doing so allows us to reframe our understanding of traumatic symptoms and the greater meaning of trauma in general. I will show that the expansion of our conception of trauma by the phenomenological viewpoint reveals facets of the experience that have previously been altogether missing.

BUILDING THE PRISM

One might wonder why not simply call the approach that I have in mind here an interdisciplinary one. While this project is certainly interdisciplinary in the most basic sense in that it brings three disciplines together, I have a specific kind of interdisciplinarity in mind which is perhaps best explained through metaphor.

We used to believe that white light was colorless. The study of optics and the willingness to look critically at our beliefs to see if they pass muster led us to the realization that white light is not colorless but contains the full spectrum of colors. Prisms work by taking in light from and through each of their surfaces, bending and shaping and separating that white light into a varied and brilliant spectrum of colors. The surfaces are connected, but do not overlap, and each are necessary for the process. The approach that I am suggesting is prismatic in a similar way—it attempts to take a particular phenomenon, examine it through three different lenses, separate the pieces and examine them critically, and then bring them back together in a unified manner that enables us to see the phenomenon in a way that is not visible through any one of the singular lenses alone. The result is an account that is as varied and brilliant and as clear as the spectrum of colors we see when we tilt a prism in the light.

Before discussing how each discipline contributes to the prismatic view, it is worth spending a moment thinking about what it is that we are looking at through the prism. We can consider trauma in at least three different ways: trauma as a disease, trauma as a sickness, and trauma as an illness. In medicine or neuroscience, the word "trauma" is used to talk about the organic pathology of PTSD. In this context, the goal of the study of trauma as disease is to understand it, catalogue its symptoms, and eradicate it. In the history of medicine or sociology, trauma is often referred to as an illness. In this context, the term spans historical epochs allowing us to talk singularly about an ailment that has had several different names over time (e.g., hysteria to battle fatigue to shell shock to post-traumatic stress). When trauma is considered as an illness, as it is in phenomenology, what is being considered is the first-person lived experience. Conceptually, the nature of trauma *as such* cannot be captured by any of these terms singularly. We can already begin to see how the prism works. Rather than looking at *just* the symptoms or organic pathology of trauma, or *just* the way that it has unfolded throughout history, or *just* the first-person lived experience, the most thorough understanding of trauma will come from an examination that brings together each of these different facets of it. The same approach should be applied to each of the three fields that studies trauma (and these three fields correspond with these terms). I will spend just a moment here explaining how I see these three disciplines as distinct pieces of a whole.

The first discipline, appropriately, is psychology. In this discipline, we can think about the way that what we now call trauma has unfolded through time as a sickness (though of course when we are speaking clinically, psychology turns to the concept of trauma as a disease). The field of psychology has been attempting to understand trauma since at least the late 1800s when Freud and Breuer published *Studies on Hysteria*. However, the designation for PTSD does not appear in the *Diagnostic and Statistical Manual of Mental Disorders* (DSM) in the United States until its third iteration in 1981. This was prompted by a large-scale study of the lasting effects of combat during and after the Vietnam War (again, an example of the disaster-model study of trauma).[4] Despite the long history of the study in psychology, just what trauma is, what counts as a traumatic event and how trauma is best treated are all still up for debate. For example, before the publication of the most recent version of the DSM, there was a debate about whether or not PTSD should be renamed "post-traumatic stress injury." Proponents of the change emphasized the fact that the symptoms of PTSD are caused by an external event or events (rather than a biologically based chemical imbalance, for example) and that there is stigma attached to being diagnosed with a disorder, which could be alleviated by a name change. Ultimately, it was decided that "injury" is simply too imprecise a word.

The second discipline is the field of neuroscience. Here we consider the experience of trauma as a disease, as neuroscience is aimed at understanding the biological mechanisms behind the traumatic response. Driven by some incredible advancements in technology, this field examines the biology of trauma to understand the mechanisms behind the symptoms of trauma that have been proffered from psychology, validating long-held theories. Think, for example, of the appearance of functional magnetic resonance imaging technology (fMRI) in the early 1990s. The use of this technology led to exciting discoveries about brain mapping, which have been directly applied to our understanding of the trauma response. Studies have suggested that when victims of trauma are shown trauma-related images, there is an increase of activity in the location of the parts of the brain thought to be related to fear and anxiety, and a decrease of activity in parts of the brain associated with working memory and executive function.[5] These studies reflect back on theories from psychology, revealing the biological basis for symptoms as well as provide possible insight into treatment methods.

It would be ludicrous to suggest that psychology and neuroscience are completely siloed from one another. Psychology has given the diagnostic framework and has also provided a rich literature of case studies that lay the theoretical foundation for understanding and recognizing trauma as well as categorizing symptoms. In response, neuroscience has developed the tools to be able to "prove" the psychological theory by finding the root of the symptom in the brain.

However, the two are sometimes at odds with one another—especially when it comes to treatment. Since neuroscience is isolating the brain as the nexus of trauma, it correspondingly often assumes that singular brain-based solutions (e.g., psychopharmaceuticals) will be the best treatment. Psychology, on the other hand, is often concerned with creating and sustaining toolboxes of evidence-based therapies that work with a wide client base. Though this may certainly include psychopharmaceuticals, it most likely does so in conjunction with other interventions. Something that they have in common is neither of the two inherently examines their own discipline through a critical, philosophical lens.

It is this critical lens that brings us to the third discipline that has attempted to understand trauma. This is a discipline that is very much siloed from the other two, and it is one that many would likely leave out when asked which fields have had the most dramatic impact on our understanding of trauma to date. This field is philosophy and specifically phenomenology.[6] Phenomenology, when aimed at the experience of trauma, provides us with four crucial points of insight that can inform the psychological and neuroscientific points of view.

Before sketching these four points, it is worth spending a moment explaining the term. The term "phenomenology" is currently used in three different ways. It may refer to the historical movement in philosophy that emphasized the study of human consciousness begun by Edmund Husserl. Second, phenomenology may refer to someone's first-personal experience, as in "the phenomenology of perception." Third, phenomenology may refer to a method of analysis that prioritizes the first-personal character of experience.[7] It is the second and third uses that are of most interest here, as my general argument is that phenomenology provides the perspective that too often goes missing when looking from the neuroscientific or psychological; namely, the first-personal perspective *as it is lived.* This is the concept of trauma as illness.

This is the first crucial insight that phenomenology provides into traumatic experience. Phenomenology—and I should be clear that I am focusing centrally on the work of Maurice Merleau-Ponty—returns us to the perspective of first-personal, conscious experience; it provides an understanding of *what it is like* to live through traumatic events, and *what it is like* to re-live those events in traumatic memory. This is not to say that psychology or neuroscience *ignores* the lived experience, but that a rich understanding of the lived experience is not the goal of psychological or neuroscientific inquiry. Rather, the patient report is gathered as data to be generalized on the way to diagnosis and treatment.

The differences can be understood more clearly by way of example. Imagine the case of someone who goes to a psychiatrist because they have lost the ability to feel enjoyment in their daily lives and do not have the energy to get out of bed. The protocol dictated by the science is to map these symptoms on to diagnostic criteria in order to find a method of treatment that ameliorates those symptoms. This is an entirely appropriate method—but can we claim to fully understand the phenomenon by abstracting from cases like this in psychiatry or psychology? No. Because a full understanding of the lived experience is not the goal in these sciences. The goal is understanding and treating symptoms.

It is critical to point out here that Merleau-Ponty's phenomenological stance is fundamentally anti-*scientism*, but it does not follow that it is anti-*science*. It is the job of phenomenology (from Merleau-Ponty's perspective) to begin from a different viewpoint, from the memory that the human being is a living, embodied, and worldly center of experience, and, as such, not simply the object of scientific inquiry. Herein lies, for Merleau-Ponty, the importance of including the phenomenological method in scientific endeavors. As he says,

> Scientific thinking, a thinking which looks on from above, and thinks of the object-in-general, *must return to the there is which precedes it*; to the site, the soil of the sensible and humanly modified world such as it is in our lives and for our bodies — . . . this actual body I call mine, this sentinel standing quietly at the command of my words and acts.[8]

Rather than take a reductive account of any human phenomena, phenomenology urges science to remember where human phenomena originate and to always return there. As he argues, "When the victim of hallucinations declares that he sees and hears, we must not believe him, since he also declares the opposite; what we must do is understand him."[9] In other words, if our goal is to grasp the experience in full, we need to step into the experience of the patient as it is lived, not abstract from the experience. The phenomenological perspective—when aimed at psychological issues—is not one that examines the patient externally with the goal of cataloguing and treating symptoms. Instead it is one that attempts to understand the phenomena *from the inside*. Again, it is not scientific investigation as such that is problematic, but the reduction of human life to causal explanations that arise from these investigations. Attempting to understand a human being as merely a biological or psychological object for scientific inquiry disregards something foundational about human existence. Though this may seem like a subtle difference, I will show that the phenomenological perspective can reframe the most prevalent features of traumatic experience in radical ways.

The second insight is that phenomenology also provides an embodiment theory, a theory that stresses the synthetic character of existence, fusing mind and body, rather than dividing them. This conception of embodiment allows for an understanding of trauma as an embodied injury, rather than one of the mind disjoined from the body or vice versa. This is especially relevant because it allows us to understand trauma as something that impacts the *entire* human being and not simply the brain. It also allows us to widen our understanding of what might be an effective treatment method. Understanding trauma to be a "bodied" problem as much as it is a "mind" problem illuminates the contours of traumatic experience more vividly, and it also explains why bodied therapies have recently been so successful in conjunction with more traditional therapeutic methods. Thinking about the human being as an embodied being also reflects back into the cognitive sciences; though we may gather important information from an fMRI scan, it is crucial to remember that human experience cannot be reduced to what we find there. There are certain important facets of experience that can never be revealed by way of a scan.

The third insight is that phenomenology allows us to see the human being as fundamentally adaptive (a view that is *not* at odds with neuroscience or psychology). This allows us to radically re-think the traumatic responses as adaptive responses to an event that have since become maladaptive or exaggerated. Indeed, in many cases, the very same adaptive responses that kept one alive in the moment of the traumatic event are those responses that become symptoms post trauma. Think, for example, of hypervigilance—a common symptom of PTSD in returning veterans. Hypervigilance—the enhanced state of sensory sensitivity—is a *desirable* trait during combat, it is one that keeps the soldier alive. This positive, lifesaving ability to adapt to a traumatic situation only becomes maladaptive when the soldier becomes unable to shut that hypervigilance off in the absence of threat. Viewing post-traumatic symptoms as rooted in positive, adaptive survival responses allows us to radically rethink the nature of PTSD as something borne of strength and survival, rather than a sign of weakness or disorder.

The phenomenological perspective allows us to reframe and better understand some of the central facets of trauma and PTSD. Beyond this, it also allows us to see aspects that we might have entirely missed—which enables us to add layers to our understanding of PTSD toward a more comprehensive account. For the past century, trauma studies across disciplines have all assumed that the ghost of a singular traumatic event haunts the sufferer. To be sure, this is a part of the problem. However, with Merleau-Ponty's emphasis on meaning and perception, we can see that those who suffer from trauma are *also* haunted by the specter of a world without meaning. Put another way, phenomenology reveals that what is injured in trauma is not simply the mind or the body but the *entire worldview of the individual*. It is this aspect of the injury—the intractable loss of one's blueprint of the world—that is missing from accounts in psychology and neuroscience. Indeed, though he did not use this term, Merleau-Ponty's phenomenology is prismatic. He brings together psychology and the sciences with phenomenology in order to reframe our understanding of human experience. Though he stands solidly in the realm of philosophy, he recognizes that no single perspective will capture the entirety of any human experience.

THE HISTORY OF TRAUMA TREATMENT: A CAUTIONARY TALE

For the skeptics who think that philosophy has no place in scientific endeavors, let us return, momentarily, to what happens when we ignore the lived experience, when we fail to take the prismatic approach.

After World War I, clinicians struggled to understand and treat what had recently been termed "shell shock." Some—but not all—soldiers were coming home with a glassy look in their eyes (called the thousand-yard stare), unable to walk or speak, obviously in great distress. At first, it was theorized that perhaps these soldiers had sustained concussions from shell blasts and that this had resulted in some sort of brain injury, hence the term "shell shock." Once this was investigated and no source of brain injury could be found, it was assumed that suffering soldiers were struggling instead with bouts of weakness.

In other words, shell shock was thought to be simply a result of human failure. Those who were stricken were assumed to be lazy, exaggerating their symptoms for sympathy. This belief led to treatments that used humiliation and violence to "snap" soldiers out of their altered states and to turn them back into heroic men. Lewis Yealland, a Canadian psychiatrist, was a proponent of such treatment. The clinician would either utter provocative statements to the patient, which would elicit an angry response or surprise him with loud noises, which would shock him out of his silence. If neither of these methods worked, a spatula would be pushed into the back of the throat. The most severe cases were treated by the application of strong electric shocks directly to the throat.[10]

In a case study published in Yealland's *Hysterical Disorders of Warfare*, Yealland describes patient A1 as someone whose mutism did not succumb to several types of treatment. After *nine months* of treatment that included intense electric shocks applied to his throat, cigarettes extinguished on his tongue, and hot plates placed at the back of his throat, patient A1 remained mute. Yealland reports that, determined to heal the patient, he told him, "You will not leave this room until you are talking as well as you ever did; no, not before . . . you must behave as the hero I expect you to be."[11]

Yealland then applied an electric shock to the throat so strong that it sent the patient reeling backwards, snapping the battery from the machine. Yealland strapped the patient down to avoid the gurney from shooting down the hallway and continued to apply shock for an hour, at which point patient A1 finally whispered "Ah." After another *hour*, the patient began to cry and whispered, "I want a drink of water."

Yealland interpreted this breakthrough to mean that his theory was correct and that his technology worked. This "success" also reflected back onto the theory, "proving" that shell shock was a disease of manhood rather than an illness that came from witnessing, being subjected to, and partaking in incredible violence. What is most chilling about reading *Hysterical Disorders of Warfare* is that there is no reticence. There is no hesitation whatsoever. There is not even the tiniest ounce of doubt that he may be wrong, or that his methods might use a critical eye. Yealland is entirely sure that his methods are effective, his theory is airtight, and the evidence is there to support it.

We like to think that we are distant, distant relatives of Yealland; that we would never engage in a therapeutic intervention as cruel and harmful. We have, after all, made much progress theoretically and technologically. However, the mistake of trusting the hard sciences without the benefit of a critical eye leaves us vulnerable to making the same mistakes—if only with different content.

It is possible that particularly in the area of treating combat trauma, we are closer cousins with Yealland than we might think. Take, for example, the use of Prolonged Exposure Therapy (PE), which is currently considered the "gold standard" for the treatment of combat-related PTSD by the US Department of Veterans Affairs. The therapy involves the patient telling and re-telling the story of their trauma over and over again in great detail until the memory loses its intense negative "charge." Though there has been some data to show that this method is successful, that data doesn't tell the whole story (no data set can do that). Further, there is a story about the development of PE that is not often told. It is a story that casts a shadow on its efficacy for combat veterans in general.

The biggest problem is what happens when PE is *not* successful. While it has helped some veterans, it has re-traumatized a significant number of other veterans. It also has an *unprecedentedly* high dropout rate—which some researchers estimate to be 50 percent, the highest dropout rate of any PTSD therapy that has been studied thus far.[12] Those who have spoken out against it publicly have been quickly cast aside in favor of the side of data that suggests success.[13]

We are no longer shocking veterans in the throat. This does not necessarily mean that we have our relationship between technology, diagnostics, and treatment figured out. This is why we need to do what Merleau-Ponty suggests in any scientific endeavor, which is always "return to the lived experience." Not because the first-personal account is the *only* relevant account, but because it should always be counted as *a* relevant account. No singular perspective tells the whole story or contains the only truth. In Yealland's case, we see directly the kind of harm that a reductionist view can have, as the firsthand, lived experience is jettisoned in favor of the data—which is seen as the one and only truth. The phenomenological perspective, then, not only allows us to rethink trauma, but provides a critical eye toward current treatment models and ensures that they remain attuned to the people being treated.

This work of understanding psychological trauma and adaptation through a prismatic and phenomenological lens is so urgently important because it will transform our definition of trauma. Not only will we be able to better understand the victim of combat trauma, but having a prismatic, three-dimensional account will at least make us aware of our blind spots, so that in a century's time, historians are not writing about us the way they now write about Yealland.

THE ROADMAP

There is much to consider here, and clearly it is impossible to do it all in one book. The general goal of the book is to build the prismatic approach, and then to bring that prismatic approach to bear on several aspects of trauma—both in the examination of the way that we understand it and also in the examination of the way that we treat it. Traumatic symptoms in general can be reframed under this approach, which expands our understanding in ways that have not yet been considered and also helps demystify and destigmatize them.

Chapter 1 has two goals. The first is to lay out some relevant facts about the history of the study of trauma in each of the three disciplines considered here. Rather than attempt to provide an exhaustive history of the study of trauma, the goal here is to begin to see the way that these three disciplines can interface with one another. The second goal of this chapter is to motivate my claim that the phenomenological lens is necessary to our understanding of combat trauma in general. I do this by highlighting some of the ways that the phenomenological lens can reframe the history of the study of trauma.

Chapter 2 brings all three disciplines to bear on what I argue is the central symptom of trauma—traumatic memory. Once again, we will see that these fields can coexist and better our understanding of trauma, and once again we will see just how critical phenomenology is in this process.

Chapter 3 shifts focus back out to traumatic experience in general, arguing that the prismatic approach allows us to see that traumatic symptoms are a natural response borne of the impulse to adapt rather than indications of disorder. Though they certainly cause distress, these symptoms are not a sign of weakness. Reframing combat trauma in this way allows us to see it as a set of distressing symptoms that is borne of strength, not weakness. This is so crucial because reframing PTSD in this way stands to change the societal stigma as well as our treatment methodologies.

Chapter 4 closes the circle on the history of typical therapeutic interventions by considering some of the ways in which current treatment interventions exacerbate, rather than help combat trauma. By examining philosophical viewpoints on the role of narrative in selfhood, I examine the benefits of narrative therapy and pull apart current deployments of that method.

Chapter 5 examines new ways forward, by specifically looking at what it means to be haunted by one's past. I suggest that over and above the typical ghost that we imagine—that of the specific traumatic memory—the veterans are also haunted by a different ghost: the specter of a world without meaning. Reframing in this way—though it may feel more abstract and perhaps even dire—allows us to finally reach PTSD at its roots. Here I suggest that empathetic response —from all of us—is the way that we can all "do our bit" to "keep the nation fighting fit."

NOTES

1. Imperial War Museums Archive, "The Cost of the Common Cold and Influenza," accessed August 24, 2018. http://www.iwm.org.uk/collections/item/object/31960.
2. Sigmund Freud and Josef Breuer, *Studies on Hysteria*, trans. Nicola Luckhurst (London: Penguin, 2004), 40–41.
3. Janet Kemp and Robert Bossarte, "Suicide Data Report, 2012," Department of Veterans Affairs Mental Health Services Suicide Prevention Program (2013), http://www.va.gov/opa/docs/Suicide-Data-Report-2012-final.pdf. See also Janet Kemp, "Suicide Rates in VHA Patients through 2011 with Comparisons with Other Americans and Other Veterans through 2010," Veterans Health Administration (2014), http://www.mentalhealth.va.gov/docs/Suicide_Data_Report_Update_January_2014.pdf.
4. Wilbur Scott, "PTSD in the DSM III, a Case in the Politics of Diagnosis and Disease," *Social Problems* 37, no. 3 (1990): 294–310.
5. Ranjedra Morey, et al., "The Role of Trauma-related Distractors on Neural Systems for Working Memory and Emotion Processing in Posttraumatic Stress Disorder," *Journal of Psychiatric Research* 43, no. 8 (2009): 809–817.
6. For an excellent article on the benefits that the phenomenological viewpoint can bring to psychology, see Kevin Aho, "Medicalizing Mental Health: A Phenomenological Alternative," *Journal of Medical Humanities* 29, no. 4 (2008): 243–259.
7. See Daniel O. Dahlstrom, Andreas Elpidorou, and Walter Hopp, *Philosophy of Mind and Phenomenology: Conceptual and Empirical Approaches* (New York: Taylor & Francis, 2015), 1–2.
8. Maurice Merleau-Ponty, "Eye and Mind," trans. Carleton Dallery, in *The Primacy of Perception: And Other Essays on Phenomenological Psychology, the Philosophy of Art, History, and Politics*, ed. James M. Edie, authored by Maurice Merleau-Ponty (Evanston, IL: Northwestern University Press, 1964), 160.
9. Maurice Merleau-Ponty, *Phenomenology of Perception*, trans. Colin Smith (New York: Routledge, 1962), 161.
10. Lewis Yealland, *Hysterical Disorders of Warfare* (London: Macmillan, 1918), 3–5.
11. Ibid.
12. Lisa Najavits, "The Problem of Dropout from 'Gold Standard' PTSD Therapies," *F1000 Prime Reports* 7, no. 43 (2015). http://doi.org/10.12703/P7-43.
13. For example, David J. Morris, *The Evil Hours: A Biography of Post-Traumatic Stress Disorder* (New York: Mariner Books, 2016).

Chapter 1

From Hysteria to PTSD

Tracing the Roots of Trauma

It is commonly thought that once we progress far enough past certain moments in scientific or technological history, the moment closes up, and so we no longer need to glance back and reflect on our successes or our failures. However, it is a misconception to believe that scientific progress supersedes historical concerns. We assume, for example, that we have progressed beyond Yealland's cruel treatment of veterans, and the hypothesis behind it, and so what use is his *Hysterical Disorders of Warfare* beyond a mere historical artifact?

A close examination of the history of the study of trauma reveals not just what we once did wrong, but also what we have inherited and imported into our current understanding of trauma. We can leave Yealland behind, but how can we be sure we have entirely exorcized his ideas and methods from our current treatment protocols? The answer is this: if we turn a blind eye to the history of the study of trauma—we *cannot* be sure. Reviving the history of the study of trauma is the only way that we can have a clear vision of why we are where we are now, of what we have inherited from the past, and of what still needs exorcizing.

In this chapter, I trace the roots of the history of trauma in the fields of psychology and neuroscience, and then make the argument that the phenomenological viewpoint, though it is not typically brought into conversation in trauma studies, allows us to expand our understanding of both the history of trauma studies and the nature of traumatic experience itself. Rather than providing a simple historical survey, I will look at the ways in which the history of our understanding of trauma reverberates in our understanding today in problematic ways.

THE ROOTS OF TRAUMA—TRAUMA AS SICKNESS

What we now call post-traumatic stress finds its origins in a different name—hysteria—which is thought to originate in Ancient Egypt. Depressive symptoms and seizures in women at this time were believed to be the result of a wandering uterus. The term "hysteria" is often credited to Hippocrates in Ancient Greece.[1] He believed that if women were not sexually active, their uterus (since it was not fulfilling its biological function) became the source of hysterical symptoms such as anxiety, tremors, convulsions, and paralysis. The cure was sexual activity, which would restore women—biologically and psychologically—to their rightful selves. Throughout the Middle Ages and the Renaissance, there were arguments about whether abstinence or sexual activity was the better cure, but the symptoms (depression, anxiety, paralysis, seizure) and the idea that the ailment originated in the female reproductive organs remained unchanged.[2]

It is worth noting that at this time these symptoms were believed to occur in women only. This idea of this kind of strictly female madness that was tied directly to the uterus and had something to do with sexuality and/or sexual activity persisted up until Pierre Janet and Jean-Martin Charcot in the late 1800s. While studying hysteria and hypnosis, the two became interested in the most intractable cases of mental illness, hysterical women, and in their studies came to the conclusion that the origin of hysteria was more complicated and could not be assumed to be caused by a lack of sexual activity[3] (van der Hart and Horst 1989).

The late 1800s in Europe saw an intense fascination with hysteria in general. Over 20 percent of all psychiatric dissertations in the late nineteenth century focused on hysteria in one sense or another, a percentage this high has not since been replicated on any other subject.[4] Charcot and Janet had taken the hysterical patient from the annals of the insane asylums and given them legitimacy. Charcot's research became well known to the public, as he held frequent Tuesday night lectures in which he would bring the hysterical patient to the stage to display her symptoms for scrutiny and discussion.[5] Charcot brought hysterical patients into the psychiatric landscape and helped redefine them as treatable, legitimate patients. Though they may have jettisoned the idea that the symptoms originated in the uterus, hysteria was still considered to be an illness that befell women exclusively.

Charcot was primarily interested in documenting hysteria and cataloguing its symptoms, but Janet, Freud, and Josef Breuer (along with others) were determined to discover the cause of the disorder. In 1893, Freud and Breuer together published "On the Psychical Mechanism of Hysterical Phenomena: Preliminary Communication," in which they theorized that the cause of hysteria was past trauma. The first example they refer to is a hypothetical one in which an upsetting emotion experienced during a dinner leads to persistent stomach upset.

> We may take as a very commonplace instance a painful emotion arising during a meal but suppressed at the time, and then producing nausea and vomiting which persists for months in the form of hysterical vomiting. (1895, 4)

The basic idea here is that when the emotions are suppressed, they do not disappear, but instead become chronic symptoms. Breuer and Freud discovered that the patient seemed to trace the discussion back to a precipitating traumatic event or series of events that were too emotionally overwhelming to process at the time they were experienced. This evidence led them to their etiological theory: an inability to cognitively process an event because of an excess of emotions leads to chronic somatic symptoms. What cannot be processed in the mind takes hold of the body. This theory led to the hypothesis that if one could process the original trauma and give voice to the initially suppressed emotions, the symptoms would then cease.

Working separately, Pierre Janet came to the same conclusion that hysterical symptoms could be associated with past traumas. He was the first to connect the theory of dissociation to traumatic memories, which explained the altered state of consciousness that hysterical patients were often found to experience. He also noticed that patients who had experienced trauma in the past would often respond differently to situations in the present. A loud banging noise might regularly elicit severe and disproportionate anxiety or anger in a hysterical patient, whereas the nonhysterical individual would find the noise unremarkable. His resulting theory was very similar to Freud and Breuer's. Janet speculated that intense emotions have an effect on the mind's ability to process an event and they lead to a different kind of memory—one that is somatic rather than cognitive, and is manifested in dreams, hyperaroused states, and dissociative states.

Had the history of trauma continued to proceed as fruitfully as it began in the 1890s, there is no telling how far the study might have progressed. However, the promising field came to a screeching halt almost as soon as it had begun for all three theorists. Charcot's work faced scrutiny when it was suggested that the subjects of his Tuesday night lectures were acting rather than experiencing true symptoms. Freud rejected his own work in 1897 and Breuer fled from the study of hysteria after a patient became intensely attached to him. Freud and Breuer abandoned their patients' mid-treatment, repudiated their own work, and the study of trauma fell out of favor.[6]

The history of the study of trauma in neuroscience also begins with hysteria. Charcot believed that the symptoms could be traced to a physical abnormality somewhere in the nervous system; a lesion or tumor somewhere in the nervous system must be to blame for hysterical symptoms. The problem with this theory was that neurologists could not find any lesions, tumors, or other physical sources of the disease. The lack of physical evidence to support Charcot's theory became "the problem of the missing lesion." This is one of the reasons why Charcot's research into hysteria eventually yielded a catalogue of symptoms rather than the discovery of a cause.[7]

Though our psychological understanding of trauma is in many ways indebted to early neuroscience, the isolated study of the brains of traumatized individuals did not occur until very recently.[8] The fact that a strong correlation could not be drawn between the physical brain and the symptoms of hysteria led to the belief that hysteria and later post-traumatic stress were primarily psychological problems and not neurological ones.[9] In fact, much of the research that has contributed to theories about the traumatized brain has been specifically focused not on the problem of PTSD itself, but rather on how the brain functions in relation to emotions in general, and more specifically those of fear and anxiety, for example, the way that fear responses are learned. This research has then been applied to victims of trauma and later combined with technological advances in neuroimaging, leading the way for theories about the way that the brain is implicated in the initial traumatic event, in subsequent traumatic symptoms, and in adaptations to these symptoms.

TRAUMA AND THE BRAIN—TRAUMA AS DISEASE

In order to talk about the way that trauma impacts the brain, it is necessary to briefly discuss some of the most basic mechanisms. This is not at all meant to be an exhaustive account of brain systems but a rough blueprint of some of the biological processes involved.

Very generally speaking, the nervous system—which includes the brain, spinal cord, peripheral nervous systems, and so on—is thought to be a system that enables us to maintain relative homeostasis in our internal environments so that we can survive in a variety of different contexts and external environments.[10] It has been theorized that there are three interdependent systems in the brain that enable this process. The first is the brain stem and the hypothalamus, which are tasked with maintaining internal equilibrium (e.g., body temperature). The second is the limbic system, thought to be in charge of regulating the balance between internal and external states (e.g., emotions and memories seem to be regulated by the limbic system).[11] The third is the neocortex, which manages our interactions with the outside world (e.g., sensory perception, language). In our normal everyday lives, we receive signals from the external world (and from our internal states).[12] Those signals are received by the brain, which is then tasked with choosing an appropriate response, initiating that response, and then terminating the response when appropriate.[13]

As we develop, given that we are biologically striving for a state of consistency and balance (homeostasis), we learn to behave more or less predictably based on exposure to certain stimuli. Our ability to discern between a variety of types of stimuli enables us to respond efficiently and effectively to the world. According to the neuroscientific perspective, then, we might think of emotions very generally as conditioned responses of the nervous system to stimuli.[14]

In the case of PTSD, it is theorized that the traumatic event causes the interruption of normal brain activity in regard to the way that memories are created. Since it is not practical to do these imaging studies during the traumatic event (or even immediately afterward), they are often done by examining the way a patient responds to cues that trigger the memory of the disaster and abstracting from that (so what we know about trauma and the brain is really about traumatic memory and the brain). If the brain responds a certain way to a visual cue from the event, it is reasonable to assume that the brain responds similarly during the actual event. Specifically, neuroimaging studies have shown that when traumatic memories are triggered by visual or aural cues, activity in portions of the brain thought to control the fear response are heightened, while activity in portions of the brain thought to be connected with translation of experiences into language are significantly decreased.[15] What this suggests is that traumatic memories are primarily somatic, rather than semantic, and that when an individual with PTSD is reminded of the traumatic event or events, they relive the event rather than remember it. This can occur as a result of fear conditioning or as a result of the way that traumatic memory becomes coded in the brain, or some combination of the two. From a neurobiological perspective, when someone has PTSD, what has been altered is the ability to maintain homeostasis.[16] Part of what is contributing to the symptomatology of PTSD is that the traumatic event or events have interrupted the brain's capacity to organize and respond to external stimuli.

Touching back to the history of trauma, what we see here is that what Freud and Breuer believed about hysteria is supported by neuroscientific research—namely, that a shocking, threatening, or overwhelming experience could lead to chronic somatic symptoms. Though the way they treated their patients was certainly ethically problematic, this does not mean that their corresponding theories were incorrect.

In this way, it is clear that the psychological and neuroscientific understandings of trauma and PTSD can complement one another. Neuroscience reveals that our emotional responses are not necessarily consciously controlled. This may seem like a minor detail, but it has two important applications to our understanding of PTSD. First, it delegitimizes claims that those who suffer from PTSD are weak willed or lazy, because we see that prior to treatment, they do not have control over their response. Second, it helps us understand how the traumatic response causes disruptive symptoms in the body even when the subject is not specifically thinking about the past event.

When it comes to healing from trauma, the neuroscientific research about the way the brain works is also relevant. It used to be the case that individuals with a PTSD diagnosis were thought to be hopeless. It is easy to see how that is the case even with the limited information here. If the traumatic response is automatic and not conscious, how can it possibly be stopped? It is thought that the answer may partially lie in what we already know about trauma. The fact that the brain can respond immediately to an incredible variety of external stimuli and then later reassess and assign meaning to those stimuli using logical and rational thought shows that a key part of brain function has to do with adaptation and flexibility. If the fear response can be conditioned, it is perhaps possible that the brain can also be conditioned to adapt to trauma.[17]

Though emotional responses can be automatic and somewhat out of our conscious control, it does not necessarily follow that once traumatized an individual remains permanently so. The rational part of the brain is not entirely subordinate to the emotional system. Instead, they exist in a dynamic relationship, each informing the other. If we can draw on the potential capacity for changeability of the brain matter that we can see in brain development (neuroplasticity), we may find that we have more control over the traumatic response than we think.

THE PHENOMENOLOGY OF TRAUMA—TRAUMA AS ILLNESS

It is a given that psychology and neuroscience should have a say when it comes to what PTSD is and how best to treat it. It is not a given that phenomenology should get to have a say. I will argue that it should for two reasons. First because it adds a layer of understanding that is not present in the psychological and neurobiological accounts, and second because this layer of understanding is not at odds with these accounts. At times it may help us reframe the way that we understand trauma, but this does not mean that it undoes the work done in psychology or neuroscience.

As we have just seen, the psychological and neuroscientific perspectives on trauma typically center on cataloguing, explaining, and alleviating *symptoms*. For the most part, they are based upon a fundamental understanding that trauma-related disorders are a set of symptoms to be treated. Though these perspectives are essential, there is a risk inherent in viewing human experience solely through the scientific/clinical lens. This risk lies in reducing human experience and behavior to what can be explained scientifically. It is certainly the case that psychological and biological systems are in play when someone is traumatized or reliving a traumatic memory. It is also vitally important to try and understand what those systems are and how they work in the presence of traumatic stress.

However, to *reduce* human experience to a series of predictable behaviors or a series of automatic responses is to ignore the importance of meaning, which I will argue is central to both the initial trauma and to the healing process. It is to ignore the first person yet contextual perspective of lived experiences, which is vitally important when it comes to understanding any human phenomena, perhaps especially trauma. Before plunging into the phenomenology of combat trauma, it is worth spending some time unpacking some central phenomenological tenets to get a better grasp of what phenomenology does.

MERLEAU-PONTY'S PHENOMENOLOGY

In the preface to the *Phenomenology of Perception*, Merleau-Ponty begins with the question, "What is phenomenology?" Situating himself among those who founded and yet did not explicitly define phenomenology, Merleau-Ponty sets this task for himself. His definition is as follows.

> Phenomenology is the study of essences . . . the essence of perception, or the essence of consciousness, for example. But phenomenology is also a philosophy which puts essences back into existence, and does not expect to arrive at an understanding of man and world from any starting point other than that of their facticity.[18]

Rather than moving away from experience and toward what can be generalized, phenomenology aims to give an account of "space, time and the world *as we 'live' them.*"[19] The phenomenological stance holds that to understand or to give an account of human existence requires a return to the world as human beings experience it, rather than dealing only with the experience of the world that has been analyzed or crafted into data. To this end, one of the central tasks that Merleau-Ponty gives to phenomenology is to provide a way of describing human experience without reducing it to mere causal explanation or scientific data.

In this way, phenomenology can be seen, at least in part, as a movement away from Cartesian dualism. Cartesian dualism draws a sharp distinction between the mind and body and creates a hierarchy within the split: the mind is of primary importance because it is the seat of the subject, whereas the body is a mere object, another thing in the world to observe and quantify. If the mind is the primary thing of which an individual can have clear and distinct knowledge (as Descartes argues in his *Meditations*), then the reflective mind becomes the framework for the entire human experience.

According to Merleau-Ponty, the seed that Descartes planted blossomed into a set of philosophical beliefs that are grounded in two deeply problematic ideas. I will consider the first here, and the second in the next section.

The first is that the mind *is* really distinct from the body and the body is of secondary importance. Merleau-Ponty argues that we don't simply *have* bodies, but that we are *embodied.* To draw a divide between mind and body is to subsequently hold that the mind is the place of the subjective world, and that the body is a part of the objective world. The second is that we arrive at truth only through scientific or intellectual analysis of experience rather than experience itself.

Let us first consider this idea of the mind and the body being inseparable. What Merleau-Ponty is worried about in Descartes's conception is that it makes the body into decaying flesh that is only accessible through specific, conscious deliberation. Take for example the experience of getting a mosquito bite. If we take Descartes literally and assume that the mind is really distinct from the body, then being bitten by a mosquito is not enough to elicit scratching. You must consciously realize that you have been bitten, and then look to your body to find the bite, and then decide to scratch it. Merleau-Ponty points out that this is not at all what this experience looks like in the lived world. If you get stung by a mosquito, you do not address your body as if it were an objective piece of the world distinct from the mind and you do not need to go looking for the bite as you might look for a dent in your car.

> [Rather, you] find it straight away, because . . . there is no question of locating it in relation to the axes of coordinates in objective space, but of reaching with the phenomenal hand a certain painful spot on [the] phenomenal body. . . . The operation takes place in the domain of the phenomenal; it does not run through the objective world . . . *quite simply he is his body and his body is the potentiality of a certain world.*[20]

Though we can certainly abstract from lived experience and talk about a thought we had yesterday, or a mosquito bite we had last summer, it is critical to understand that this is an abstraction—and therefore not equivalent to the lived experience. Consciousness *cannot* be split from the body, it depends on and extends throughout the body and, through the body, to the external world, with which it is in constant interplay. We engage with the external world through our experience as embodied beings whose world is presented and shaped not simply for and by the mind, but also the "natural system of one's own body."[21] According to Merleau-Ponty, it is untenable to separate the mind from the body because "the body is our general medium for having a world."[22]

To give an example from the *Phenomenology of Perception* that is more intimately connected to traumatic experience, Merleau-Ponty considers a case in which a young woman who has been forbidden from seeing the man that she loves loses her ability to speak. He argues that her inability to speak is *not* conscious or chosen. She is not consciously performing and acting out as one might think, rather her consciousness is extending through her bodily interaction with the world. She cannot speak because the way that she typically interacts with the world has been interrupted.

This understanding of her symptoms originates from his conception of embodied consciousness. As he explains,

> The body does not constantly express the modalities of existence in the way that stripes indicate rank, or a house-number a house: the sign here does not only convey its significance, it is filled with it; it is, in a way, what it signifies.[23]

The action does not convey a secret message from the brain, the action is *filled* with significance—the girl's muteness is not a symptom of her trauma, it *is* her trauma. The body is not a puppet responding to orders from the brain; the real meaning of our actions is not revealed when we understand what is going on neurologically. Rather, consciousness and body *coexist* in the human being and inform one another. The body does not stand for or represent what is happening in consciousness, it is a vital *part* of consciousness. This is why individual meaning then becomes essential in understanding trauma and developing adaptive methods for treating it. Bodily symptoms—though we may be able to trace their origins to specific regions in the brain—are not reducible to those regions.

To be sure, there are situations in which it is helpful (and necessary) to isolate a specific part of the brain or body in order to treat it. What is critical to understand is that when we do this, we can no longer claim to grasp the phenomenon in its entirety. To give a trivial example, though it is important to directly treat a break in the arm in a reductionist manner (e.g., isolating which bone is fractured and how badly, determining whether pins are necessary or if a cast will be sufficient, following a treatment protocol), this treatment deals only with the break, it *cannot* capture all of the other aspects of healing (e.g., what it means to break your wrist, what it is like to be restrained in a cast for six weeks, how such a small problem can reverberate through each aspect of your life from going to work to showering or washing dishes, how strange it can be to lose muscle in that arm).

When we fail to take account of individual meaning and operate on the assumption that science *does* capture the entire phenomenon, we not only miss potentially important aspects of the experience, but risk getting our treatment protocol wrong. Recall the treatment implemented by Lewis Yealland detailed in the prologue. Yealland, and many others, believed that the brutal treatment of soldiers was successfully shocking traumatized soldiers back into themselves. This belief is based on the hypothesis behind the treatment, which was that these symptoms did not indicate a true problem, but instead represented weakness—manifested in the expression of self that needed to be replaced by the real self, the heroic self, the true self.

In detailing a particularly productive morning, Yealland claims that he treated six mute patients in the space of a half an hour. The first patient responded to loud coughing in his ear, the next to the forcing of a tongue depressor to the back of his throat, the next three to strong electric shocks to their throats; and "the sixth, on hearing the others fell from a chair, striking his head on the floor, and began to talk."[24] Yealland thought that he had returned the soldiers to their real state of being (the heroic, moral, true state) when they began to speak in response to his treatment. He believed that brutality was not only justifiable, but a necessary means of reaching the puppet master behind the pathological symptoms. What is perhaps more likely is that the brutal treatment created new and vivid *meaning* for the soldier in and through his body: speak now or continue to submit yourself to bodily harm. The sixth soldier fell out of his chair and began to speak, perhaps not because he had been cured, but because he had been terrified.

This highlights precisely what Merleau-Ponty was worried about. Namely, when we *reduce* human phenomena to the necessarily generic perspective of a scientific explanation, we risk a detrimental oversimplification that—as we see in the case of Yealland—can come to bear on treatment. To separate the mind from the body as if they are two distinct entities is to risk missing what the experience (and treatment) means to the individual, and something important about what it means to exist in the world as a bodied being. This brings us to the second problematic idea from Descartes.

CRITIQUES OF SCIENTISM AND REFLECTION

The second (and related) problematic idea that rose from Cartesian dualism is the idea that we arrive at truth only through scientific or intellectual analysis of experience rather than experience itself. Put in another way, this is the idea that the truth of the human condition lies in *reflection* upon existence, rather than in the *experience* of existence itself. Merleau-Ponty argues that reflection upon experience does not give way to the objective truth of that experience. There is the experience of the event, and then there is reflection upon that experience—and it is dangerous to conflate these two things.

Instead, reflection and analysis of experience give way to scientific data, which again, is important, but does not give an exhaustive account of any phenomena *as it is lived*. The view that the truth of human experience is gained from reflection and analysis is problematic because it treats the world as fodder for scientific experiment and nothing further. It takes "the scientist's knowledge as if it were absolute, as if everything that is and has been was meant only to enter the laboratory."[25] It is presumptuous—and, for the understanding and treatment of trauma, dangerous—to assume that the scientific viewpoint on any human phenomena is the *only* legitimate one. To assume this is to banish lived experience in favor of scientific explanations of experience.

The Müller-Lyer optical illusion provides a simple example of Merleau-Ponty's point (see figure 1.1). In this illusion, two lines appear to be two different lengths, because the fins on one arrow point inward, while the fins on the other arrow point outward.

The first time you encounter this vision, you might report that the arrow with outward facing fins is longer than the other arrow. We can label this is perception (A). Upon reflection, you might examine the arrows more closely, perhaps measure them, and will then realize that despite appearances, the arrows are actually the same length. This experience is perception (B).

According to Merleau-Ponty, we make a mistake when we assume that perception (B)—which includes the analysis of perception (A)—is simply a *corrected* version of perception (A). They are, in fact, two entirely distinct perceptual experiences. The kind of analytical reflection that is necessary in perception (B) does not make perception (A) *incorrect*; it provides us with an entirely new perceptual experience. "Reflection," then, does not make fuzzy perceptions more clear, it does not bring us to the objective truth of the world, rather it "obscures what we thought was clear."[26] At the time of perception (A), you may have been unaware that the perception was an illusion. If, after reporting that the arrow with the outward facing fins is longer than the other arrow, someone were to ask, "Are you *sure*?" You become unsure of your statement. What you thought was clear is now obscured. The subsequent discovery that the arrows are the same length does not *correct* perception (A) but provides a *new* perception altogether.

Further, assessing the accuracy of perception (A) and perception (B) does not touch the *experience* of perceiving these two lines. Perceiving and analyzing perception are two different acts. As Merleau-Ponty remarks, "The two straight lines . . . are neither of equal or unequal length; it is only in the objective world that this question arises."[27] Perception is not, then, inherently oriented toward objective accuracy. The analysis of perception does not

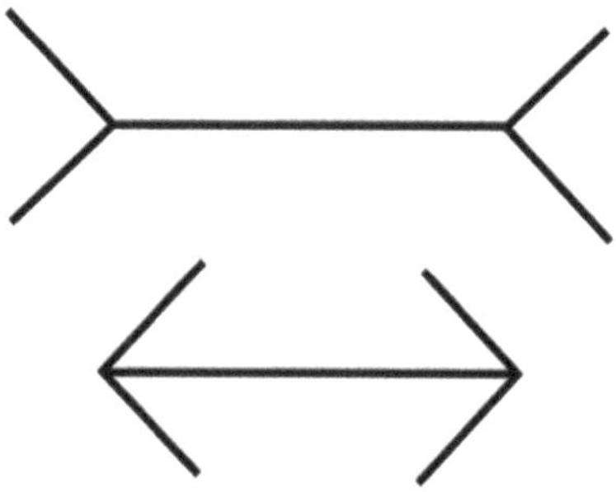

Figure 1.1 An example of the Müller-Lyer illusion.

ensure that our perception is more accurate. Rather, it does something different, it takes perception out of the lived world and attempts to place it into the world of objective truths.

In *The Phenomenology of Perception*, perception acts as a kind of proof of the existence of a nonobjective reality as Merleau-Ponty points out numerous occasions in which perception defies reduction. In one such example, Merleau-Ponty invites the reader to imagine walking along a shore and coming upon a ship that has run aground. The ship and its masts and funnel are fixed in the objective world; they are physically there. One's individual perception of that ship, however, is much less fixed and objective. There is a point at which one is at such a distance that the perception of these pieces of the ship is not yet integrated. It might be clear that there is a ship run aground, but the masts might not yet be visible as they are buried within the perception of the forest behind them. As one approaches them, eventually "there will be a moment when these details somehow become part of the ship, and indissolubly fused with it."[28] An intellectualist variety of reductionism is inclined to explain this experience by appealing to the intellect's powers of actively analyzing and synthesizing (judging); an empiricist variety of reductionism appeals to sheer processes of association that happen to congeal into a unified entity.

What Merleau-Ponty wants to assert is that this work is done by *perception itself*; it is neither the product of an intellectual synthesis nor an imaginative association of impressions. The perception of the ship is the perception of one unified meaningful object that originally presents itself as such; it emerges neither from an analysis of a disconnected or confusing perception nor from some imaginative association of impressions. Instead, as he says, the mast and the funnel simply *become* a part of the ship at a certain point. The ship, though it may remain aground, somehow seems to *emerge* from the shore and the forest behind it as one meaningful object for perception.

This reframing done by Merleau-Ponty not only allows us to reconsider specific instances of perceptions, but also enables us to come to a new understanding of perception in general. As Merleau-Ponty explains, perception "lay[s] the foundations of, or inaugurate[s] knowledge."[29] It is the job of phenomenology, then, to begin from a different viewpoint, from the memory that the human being is a living, embodied, and worldly center of experience, and, as such, not the *object* of scientific inquiry. This, then, is where Merleau-Ponty's phenomenology begins; in the stance that there is something irreducible about human experience, what Thomas Nagel influentially dubbed the "what it is like" phenomenon, that appears to elude standard causal explanation in science, when that phenomenon is reduced, *qua explanandum*, to a calculable object.

Rather than take a reductive account of any human phenomena, phenomenology urges science to remember where human phenomena originate and to return there. It is critical to understand here that the goal is not to jettison the scientific in favor of the personal, or the objective in favor of the subjective. In fact, one of Merleau-Ponty's central ideas seems to be that these divisions are merely apparent.

TRAUMA AND PHENOMENOLOGY

Though Merleau-Ponty is not oft cited as a trauma theorist, he spent much of his time thinking and writing about Johann Schneider, a combat veteran studied by the psychologists Kurt Goldstein and Adhemar Gelb, who serves as Merleau-Ponty's primary case study in the *Phenomenology of Perception*. Though he is often critical of the way that psychology and neuroscience try to reduce Schneider's symptoms, he also treats the science and the phenomenological perspective as inherently complementary.

Numerous observations by Merleau-Ponty bear out this claim. To begin with the quote above, note that Merleau-Ponty does not suggest that scientific thinking be *replaced* by phenomenology, but rather that phenomenology can remind science of the importance of the lived experience of the subject. The *Phenomenology of Perception* contains a similar sentiment.

> I cannot conceive of myself as nothing but a bit of the world, a mere object of biological, psychological or sociological investigation. I cannot shut myself up within the realm of science. All my knowledge of the world, even my scientific knowledge, is gained from my own particular point of view, or from some experience of the world without which the symbols of science would be meaningless.[30]

In other words, what Merleau-Ponty is particularly concerned about is the regard for science as the ultimate and sole source of knowledge about human behavior. This regard concerns him because *any* knowledge of the world is, as he sees it, ultimately grounded in, as he puts it, "some experience of the world." It is not scientific investigation as such, but the reduction of human life to causal explanations that arise from these investigations that is problematic. Attempting to understand a human being as *merely* a biological or psychological object for scientific inquiry disregards something foundational about human existence. Phenomenology, then, is a body of thought aimed at shifting focus back onto the lived being as a whole.

Although the phenomenological method is distinct from those of psychology and neuroscience, this distinction does not entail that they are incompatible. Take, for example, Pavlov's dogs. Even the Pavlovian response cannot be reduced to automatic responses in the brain. Though we can explain the dogs' behavior by explaining the brain response, what is happening for the dog is not simply brain activity. Pavlov created new meaning from neutral stimuli for those dogs; to them, the noise *meant* that food was on its way. What is so compelling to the dog is not the brain activity, but the meaning that has been created around the sound and the future promise of food.[31] The phenomenological viewpoint here does not contradict the scientific one; it simply adds a new level of understanding.

Further, the claims in the *Phenomenology of Perception* are not all negative. Beyond the goal of criticizing reductionist claims, Merleau-Ponty also intends to give a positive account of perception as the fundamental basis of experience. As he explains,

> Perception is not a science of the world, it is not even an act, a deliberate taking up of a position; it is the background from which all acts stand out, and is presupposed by them.[32]

A central claim of the *Phenomenology of Perception* then is the idea that perception is not just one facet of human experience. Rather, it is the condition for the possibility of experience. Doing justice to the specific perceptual experience of any human phenomenon becomes essential if one hopes to reach a thorough understanding of that phenomenon.

The importance of Merleau-Ponty's phenomenological perspective lies in its capacity to provide important insights into any human experience that is also examined from a scientific point of view. Such a perspective zeroes in, for example, on what it is like for someone to suffer from cancer. Awareness of how cancer changes one's lived experience can impact treatment in several different ways. While the surgeon removing the tumor does not need to know how having that tumor has changed the way that the individual feels in the world in order to operate successfully, the first-person experience of having brain cancer is still valuable for care. Further, we can hardly claim to fully understand the phenomenon without considering what it is like. In order to successfully understand trauma and PTSD, it is *essential* to know what it is like for the individual who suffers from it. The phenomenological perspective allows for focus on (a) how symptoms are appearing and interrupting the victims' daily interactions with the world; (b) how overwhelming it felt and why (rather than a simple account of what the trauma entailed); and (c) what it means to have been traumatized and what it means to relive the trauma.

The difference made by the phenomenological approach to trauma becomes evident even in the simple definition of trauma. When Merleau-Ponty speaks about trauma, he defines it in terms of how it is experienced in time by the individual. "Time in its passage does not . . . close up on traumatic experience; the subject remains open to the same impossible future, if not in his explicit thoughts, at any rate in his actual being."[33] The emphasis here is not on *what happened*, but *what it was like* to experience the event from the perspective of that particular individual. A traumatic event is one which is so upsetting in that it does not fade into the past but remains somehow always in the present, rather than an event that meets certain objective criteria dictated by a psychological manual. No matter how much time passes, the event remains *meaningfully present* for the individual. This is not incompatible with the psychological definition of symptoms, but it is very careful not to reduce the experience to the impersonal level of scientific explanation.

CONCLUSION: FINDING THE LEAK

In the next chapter, I show specifically how phenomenology interfaces with psychology and neuroscience on traumatic memory—how it is complementary and how it simultaneously allows us to reframe what traumatic memory is. Before doing this, I want to motivate the use of phenomenology in the understanding of trauma in one more way by returning to a concept that I introduced in the beginning of the chapter—the mistaken belief that scientific progress supercedes historical concerns.

We tend to believe that as science progresses, we can shut certain chapters from the history of an idea completely. Return for a moment to the example of Lewis Yealland. Yealland and his methods are over one hundred years old. We have progressed both in terms of our theories behind PTSD and in our treatment of PTSD. We have come to see his treatment as cruel and unusual, and we have abandoned it. When it comes to Freud, we have abandoned his methodology—we don't even use the word "hysterical" in clinical settings anymore. What I want to suggest here is that just as time does not completely close up on traumatic events, it does not completely close up on the history of trauma either. There are still traces of Yealland and Freud in our societal and clinical conceptions of trauma, and if we do not recognize them, we will simply continue to perpetuate them.

NOTES

1. Though it was long thought that the term originated with Hippocrates, the term cannot be found in any Hippocratic writings though he did write about this kind of madness and its cure. For our purposes, the exact origin of the term is not as relevant as its continued use in the late nineteenth century.

2. Cecilia Tasca, et al., "Women and Hysteria in the History of Mental Health," *Clinical Practice and Epidemiology in Mental Health* 8, no. 1 (2012): 110–119.

3. Onno Van der Hart and Rutger Horst, "The Dissociation Theory of Pierre Janet," *Journal of Traumatic Stress* 2, no. 4 (1989): 397–412.

4. Mark S. Micale, "On the 'Disappearance' of Hysteria: A Study in the Clinical Deconstruction of a Diagnosis," *Isis* 84, no. 3 (1993): 496–526.

5. Judith Herman aptly called these Tuesday night lectures "theatrical events" that were not just attended by physicians and students, but also many other members of society who were also fascinated with hysteria. Judith Herman, *Trauma & Recovery* (New York: Basic Books, 1999), 10–11. This certainly raises the question of whether Charcot was making these hysterical patients legitimate, or further delegitimizing them by turning them into a spectacle. Setting aside questions about the ethics of his treatment of these patients, Charcot should be credited with bringing them into the psychological landscape in a new way.

6. Herman, *Trauma & Recovery,* 15–20.

7. For a thorough history of the study of hysteria, see also Ilza Veith, *Hysteria: The History of a Disease* (Chicago: University of Chicago Press, 1965).

8. There were, of course, enormous advancements being made in neuroscience in general after Charcot. Some of this research was based on victims of bodily trauma (Phineas Gage, for example). The topic of the *psychological* trauma as a neurological issue was not taken up again until after Vietnam. More recently, as an interest with neuroimaging in general has grown, and ten years of war and traumatized veterans, the number of imagining studies has increased. For details, see K. C. Hughes and L. M. Shin, "Functional Neuroimaging Studies of Post-traumatic Stress Disorder," *Expert Review of Neurotherapeutics* 11, no. 2 (2011): 275–285.

9. With the exception, of course, of traumatic brain injury that is considered to be a physical injury that is sometimes comorbid with PTSD. See, for example, David Trudeau, et al., "Findings of Mild Traumatic Brain Injury in Combat Veterans With PTSD and a History of Blast Concussion," *The Journal of Neuropsychiatry and Clinical Neurosciences* (1998): 308–313.

10. Paul MacLean, *The Triune Brain in Evolution: Role in Paleocerebral Function* (New York: Plenum, 1990).

11. The limbic system is the subject of intense debate in neuroscience. Originally, it was thought to be the center of emotion regulation and long-term memory formation. In 1990, neuroscientist Paul MacLean published an influential book called *The Triune Brain in Evolution: Role in Paleocerebral Function* in which he defended a model of the brain that developed three distinct systems in evolution. According to MacLean, the brain is made up of the reptilian complex, the paleomammalian complex (limbic system), and the neomammalian complex (neocortex). Each of these systems had a sort of position in an evolutionary hierarchy, so the reptilian complex was responsible for behavior at the instinctual level, the limbic system was responsible for behavior on a higher emotional level, and the neocortex was responsible for the highest level of behavior on the rational level. See MacLean, *Triune Brain in Evolution*, esp. 15–18 & 247–268. MacLean's triune model has since been refined, and portions of it disputed. His understanding of the limbic system has been disputed most notably by Joseph LeDoux, who believes that the term is obsolete and refers to a complicated system that is not as unified as it once appeared to be. Much of the debate centers around which sections of the brain should be included as part of the limbic system, and *not* about whether or not the limbic system plays an important role in our emotional lives. See Joseph LeDoux, "Emotion Circuits in the Brain," *Annual Review of Neuroscience* (2000): 155–184. The idea that the limbic system is at least partially responsible for the regulation of emotions and formation of memories still persists.

12. MacLean, *Triune Brain in Evolution*, 273–293.

13. Bessel van der Kolk, "Posttraumatic Stress Disorder and the Nature of Trauma," *State of the Art: Dialogues in Clinical Neuroscience* 2, no. 1 (2000): 13. See also Antonio Damasio, *Descartes' Error: Emotion, Reason, and the Human Brain* (New York: Grossett & Putnam, 1994); Jaak Panksepp, *Affective Neuroscience* (New York: Oxford University Press, 1998).

14. Emotions, of course, are much more complicated than this. There is a distinction in neuroscience between emotions that occur pre-consciously and those that are conscious. The emphasis on emotions in the neurology of trauma and PTSD is on those that are pre-conscious. This is not to say that emotions are never conscious or rational, or that they are not subject to reflection or conscious manipulation. See Joseph LeDoux, *The Emotional Brain: The Mysterious Underpinnings of Emotional Life* (New York: Simon & Schuster, 1996). See also Bessel van der Kolk, "Clinical Implications of Neuroscience Research in PTSD," *Annals of the New York Academy of Sciences* 1071 (2006): 277–293.

15. LeDoux, *The Emotional Brain*, 17.

16. Some, like Bruce McEwen, might argue that there is allostasis—a new, differently regulated state—rather than the loss of the ability to regulate homeostasis; see Bruce McEwen, "Stress, Adaptation, and Disease: Allostasis and Allostatic Load," *Annals of the New York Academy of Sciences* 840 (1998): 33–44.

17. See, for example, Ruth Lanius, Robyn Bluhm, and P. A. Frewen, "How Understanding the Neurobiology of Complex Post-traumatic Stress Disorder can Inform Clinical Practice: A Social Cognitive and Affective Neuroscience Approach," *Acta Psychiatrica Scandinavica* (2011): 331–348.

18. Merleau-Ponty, *Phenomenology of Perception*, vii.
19. Merleau-Ponty, *Phenomenology of Perception*, vii, emphasis added.
20. Ibid., 121–122.
21. Ibid., 121.
22. Ibid., 169. There is an interesting question of whether or not Merleau-Ponty has taken Descartes a bit too literally regarding his mind/body dualism. Descartes's correspondence with Elisabeth of Bohemia and subsequently his work *The Passions of the Soul* seem to suggest that perhaps Descartes was not as committed to the mind/body dualism found in the *Meditations*. See Elisabeth of Bohemia, "Correspondence to Rene Descartes," in *Women Philosophers of the Early Modern Period*, ed. Margaret Atherton (Indianapolis, IN: Hackett Publishing, 1994), 11–21; and Rene Descartes, *Meditations on First Philosophy*, trans. John Cottingham (New York: Cambridge University Press, 2013), 32–47 & 100–125. Though it may be true that Descartes's thought progressed substantially after the publication of the *Meditations*, it should be noted that Merleau-Ponty is not simply taking issue with Descartes as an individual thinker, but with the intellectualist and empiricist traditions that sprung out of his work.
23. Merleau-Ponty, *Phenomenology of Perception*, 186.
24. Yealland, *Hysterical Disorders of Warfare*, 3–4.
25. Merleau-Ponty, "Eye and Mind," 160.
26. Ibid., 12.
27. Ibid., 6.
28. Ibid., 20.
29. Ibid., 19. For an excellent discussion of what he calls Merleau-Ponty's "living perception," see Lawrence Hass's, *Merleau-Ponty's Philosophy* (Bloomington, IN: Indiana University Press, 2008), 53–70.
30. Merleau-Ponty, *Phenomenology of Perception*, ix.
31. Though a dog is obviously neurologically quite different from a human being, Merleau-Ponty would still find the interaction between the dog and the world to be a meaningful one. Though conscious meaning is not necessarily in play here, there is meaning insofar as the dog relates to the world. Merleau-Ponty uses an example of the way that an insect is affected by an injury. See Merleau-Ponty, *Phenomenology of Perception*, 90. This passage suggests that any animate being is subject to some kind of phenomenological analysis by his account.
32. Merleau-Ponty, *Phenomenology of Perception*, xi.
33. Ibid., 95.

Chapter 2

They Carry It with Them

Phenomenologies of Traumatic Memory

Regardless of the type of trauma that one sustains, the most prevalent—relentless—features of post-traumatic experience have to do with the way the event is remembered. The experience of remembering a traumatic event is psychologically, phenomenologically, and neurologically distinct from that of remembering nontraumatic events. In this chapter, I explore the nature of traumatic memory from the perspectives of psychology, phenomenology, and neuroscience, yielding an understanding of trauma that stretches from the most basic synaptic level of brain function to the lived experience itself. We will see that the phenomenological perspective adds to those of psychology and neuroscience by allowing us to consider not just what traumatic memory is as a symptom, but its significance to the subject.

I begin with the way that traumatic memory is described in psychology in order to provide a basic framework for the concept of traumatic memory as a central symptom of PTSD. Next, I move into a basic understanding of the neuroscience of memory in order to understand the mechanism of traumatic memory on the brain level, which gives a possible model to explain the mechanism of these symptoms. Finally, I consider the phenomenology of traumatic memory, which considers the experience from the first-personal, lived perspective.

Phenomenology asks what it is like to experience a certain phenomenon. What we will find is that the answer to this question provides us not only with critical information that is missing from psychological framework and the neuroscientific explanation, but an answer that leads us to a much deeper understanding of trauma and the experience of traumatic memory.[1] Indeed one that may reframe our understanding of trauma altogether.

PSYCHOLOGY AND TRAUMATIC MEMORY

The Diagnostic and Statistical Manual of Mental Disorders, currently in its fifth edition (DSM-V), organizes the symptoms of PTSD into clusters. In order to be diagnosed with PTSD, a patient has to have experienced at least one symptom from each of the clusters of symptoms for a period of longer than one month. The second cluster contains symptoms that pertain to the way that the traumatic event continues to be relived in memory.[2] According to this cluster, traumatic memories are experienced in at least one of the following ways:

1. Recurrent, involuntary, and intrusive distressing memories of the traumatic event(s).
2. Recurrent distressing dreams in which the content and/or effect of the dream are related to the traumatic event(s).
3. Dissociative reactions (e.g., flashbacks) in which the individual feels or acts as if the traumatic event(s) were recurring. (Such reactions may occur on a continuum, with the most extreme expression being a complete loss of awareness of present surroundings.)
4. Intense or prolonged psychological distress at exposure to internal or external cues that symbolize or resemble an aspect of the traumatic event(s).
5. Marked physiological reactions to internal or external cues that symbolize or resemble an aspect of the traumatic event(s).[3]

These criteria describe different ways in which the past intrudes on the present. The first criterion refers to intrusive thoughts that may break through consciousness while awake, the second to the way that the event(s) get reconstituted in dream life. The third criterion calls up situations in which the past overlaps and overtakes the present partially or completely. The fourth and fifth criteria focus on the ways that the psychological state that was characteristic of the original event can be recreated in the presence of things that remind one of the original trauma.

It is important to note that in each of these cases, the memory carries the original trauma with it in some way. As one leading trauma expert explains, "Traumatic memories [are] retrieved (at least initially) in the form of mental imprints of sensory and affective elements of the traumatic experience."[4] Traumatic events do not get recorded as neat and tidy coherent stories. Instead they exist in the mind as vivid flashes, fragments, and parts of stories that are missing elements or do not seem to follow chronological order. They carry imprints of the past into the present. The idea of a memory carrying elements of the original experience may not seem sufficient to establish a difference between traumatic and nontraumatic memories, but there are three substantial dissimilarities between traumatic and nontraumatic memories that we should notice.

First, it is important to understand that traumatic memories are retrieved *as* sensory and affective elements, not *alongside* sensory and affective elements. The implication here (discussed in further detail below) is that the traumatic memory is primarily (and sometimes only) sensory and affective and *not* available as the subject of conscious thought in the way that other memories typically are. This means that the imprint (which might be an emotion, such as a fear or a feeling of rage, or a visual memory of a complex scene or something as simple as a color) might come flooding forward without seeming to be attached to anything at all.

Second, the sensory and affective elements in traumatic memory cause *anguish*. Positive memories may carry with them elements from the past, but they do not cause anguish (unless we want to classify nostalgia as a kind of anguish). For example, one may have had a positive experience of listening to the album *Kind of Blue* for the first time in a café. Walking into a café and smelling freshly brewed coffee might lead one to start humming to tune to "So What" even years later. Alternatively, hearing "So What" may call to mind the sense memory of these smells. However, this memory is neither distressing nor is it retrieved *only* as sensory and affective fragments. It is likely (or at the very least possible) that one would be able to cognitively remember the original experience of first listening to the album and therefore understanding why the smell of coffee seems to trigger the auditory memory of the album, or why hearing the song conjures the olfactory memory of the coffee.

Third, traumatic memories are *invasive*. While the memory of the café and the music may be intense, and may appear unbidden, this memory is not intrusive in the same distressing way that traumatic memories are. As we will see below, traumatic memories can exercise intense power over normal brain function, effectively taking over the present moment. Traumatic memories, then, though they may retain some of the same features as nontraumatic memory, are distinct from nontraumatic memories in at least three ways: they are experienced as primarily sensory and affective and therefore not available cognitively, they are invariably distressing, and they are intensely intrusive.

Cases from the psychological literature can provide examples of how disruptive intrusive memories can be. Psychiatrist Jonathan Shay compiled accounts from the experience of his patients. One patient, a Vietnam veteran with PTSD, describes the way that traumatic memory intrudes on his life in the following way.

> I haven't spent a complete night in bed with my wife for at least ten years. I always end up on the sofa. It's safer for her. . . . After I couldn't work anymore

> . . . . I'd do this crazy shit at night. I once threw her out of bed so hard it broke her shoulder. I thought there was an NVA potato-masher [a grenade] come in on us. Another night I thought *she* was a Gook, and I had my hands around her throat before I woke up.[5]

The symptoms described here are consistent with criteria one, three, and four from the DSM entry above. Beyond that, though, here are several notable aspects to this report. The first is the longevity and intensity of the traumatic memory. *Ten years* after the event, the patient *still* has intense reactions that lead him to act and feel *as if* he is under attack, despite the fact that he rationally knows he is no longer in Vietnam. While a minimum duration of symptoms is specified in the DSM, it does not at all capture the way that the symptoms can permeate one's life, persisting for *decades*. His dissociation is so total that he *cannot tell* the difference between the past and the present. What this shows is that in some sense, traumatic memory is not simply memory in the sense of conscious recollection. Rather, it is a memory marked by an intense experience of reliving. As Shay puts it, "Traumatic memory is not narrative. Rather, it is experience that *reoccurs*."[6] It almost doesn't make sense to talk about it as if it were a memory, as the memory of a traumatic event causes the individual to experience the present moment *as if* it were the past. For this patient, the lines between the past and present are blurred. So vivid is the memory in the traumatized patient that he becomes entirely convinced that he and his wife are under grenade fire, or that she is an enemy combatant. Even the most intensely positive memories do not have this kind of power.

To take another example, Abram Kardiner describes the rotating nightmares of one of his patients, who had been home from war for more than eight years. One variation is as follows.

> I am in the yard while playing the water hose upon the flagstones. Water stops running. After a while it begins again. Then the neighbor from whom I borrowed the hose comes out and reproaches me, finally swears at me, and then strikes me. Then all the neighbors come running out, and they chase me all over. Then I awaken in a sweat, feeling as though I had the life pounded out of me.[7]

This account is consistent with criterion two above. Here it is notable that the subject material of the dream is not directly related to the traumatic experience of combat. Rather, here it is the effect of combat, feeling under attack, exhausted, beaten down, that is represented (and/or re-presented) in the dream. What is being re-lived here is the emotion that accompanied the original trauma rather than its content. While anyone could have a distressing dream like this one, this situation has become chronic. The patient has a distressing dream of some kind nearly every night—and has for the past eight years.

Traumatic memories are marked by relentless, persistent, invasive, and evocative instances of reliving that take hold of the present. This sets them far aside from the most vivid of nontraumatic memories. It seems possible, for example, to have quite intrusive and vivid positive memories that are experienced as some kind of reliving. The smell of freshly baked bread might bring one back to one's childhood. This memory might enact itself within the subject quite disruptively. One might imagine walking into a restaurant with a business partner for a lunch meeting and becoming thoroughly distracted by the sudden memory triggered by the smell of fresh bread, so much so that it becomes difficult to carry on the conversation without effort. However, the subject of this kind of memory will not *mistake* her business partner for her mother, the café will not *become* her childhood home. The past, though it may briefly enter into the present, does not *take over* the present. Though vivid, the memory is not relentless, violent, or upsetting. It can be referred to consciously, and it can ultimately be set aside (though it may take some effort). In traumatic memory, the past is not recollected consciously, it is instead relived in the sense that the memory carries the past somehow with it.

Psychology, then, provides an initial framework for understanding traumatic memory. The neuroscientific examination of memory presented in the next section adds more detail to this framework by sketching why traumatic memories can so forcefully take hold of the present.

NEUROSCIENCE AND TRAUMATIC MEMORY

It is far beyond the scope of this book to give a complete account of the neuroscience of traumatic memory. What I aim to do here is unpack some of the basic neurobiological processes involved in traumatic memory in order to clarify the way that traumatic memories are laid down.

Memory shapes human behavior. It is what enables us to get home each day after work, to avoid things that we learn to be dangerous, and it is central in helping us create and maintain connections with one another. As noted in the previous section, traumatic memories can become chronic symptoms, intrusive instances of reliving instead of opportunities of remembrance. It is not clear, however, *why* traumatic events tend to create memories that intrude on the present endlessly. Understanding some of the neuroscience behind the differences between traumatic and nontraumatic memories can help explain the etiology of these psychological symptoms.

It is thought that there are two systems that regulate the formation of memories in the brain.[8] The hippocampal system is responsible for encoding and possibly storing what have been termed declarative or explicit memories.

These are memories that the subject can distinctly focus her attention on, recall consciously, and refer to in thought or speech.

The amygdala system, on the other hand, is responsible for non-declarative or implicit memories that have strong emotional resonance, which are not (and sometime cannot be) consciously recollected. For example, you might have an explicit memory of going to dinner with a friend last night. This explicit memory is a distinct episode from the past that you can bring into conscious attention. If asked about the meal the next day, you would be able to focus your attention on the events of yesterday, recall what you ate for dinner, and details from the conversation that you had over the meal.[9] Implicit memories, on the other hand, are not brought into conscious attention, though they shape much of our behavior. Often, this is because these memories have been stored for so long that they do not need to be explicitly referred to. If you drove to the aforementioned dinner, it is likely that you did not have to specifically recall each lesson from driving school in order to operate your vehicle. When you looked at the menu to find something to order, it is likely that you did not have to recite the alphabet and sound out each of the words in order to understand the names of dishes. The lessons that you learned in order to drive and to read are implicit and do not need to be brought into consciousness in order to shape behavior.

These two systems can operate relatively independently. In a well-known case, Édouard Claparède, a French doctor, demonstrated this condition by experimenting on a patient with amnesia. Claparède's patient could not form new conscious memories. Each time she met with the doctor, he had to re-introduce himself to her, and she had no memory of their previous conversations. One day, Claparède greeted her with a tack in his hand that pricked her when they shook hands. The next day, though the patient still did not consciously remember Claparède, she refused to shake his hand, and continued to refuse to do so despite never being able to remember why.[10] This patient was physically incapable of creating an explicit memory that would allow her to remember being pricked in the hand by Claparède's tack. *And yet*, she still somehow knew not to shake his hand. Though she could not call into consciousness the memory of being pricked with the pin, the memory was implicitly operating somewhere in her mind and shaping her behavior.

Research like this has led neuroscientists to theorize that the amygdala system is responsible for implicit memories that have emotional content, while the hippocampal system is responsible for explicit memories that do not have felt emotional content.

Even if there presumably are two different memory systems that can operate independently of one another, this does not mean that implicit and explicit memories are mutually exclusive. There are many ways in which our implicit and explicit memories coincide. For example, if when you went to dinner with your friend you had a terrible argument that ended your friendship, you likely have both explicit and implicit memories of this. When explaining what happened the next day, you can consciously bring the event into your mind and describe details about the meal and the conversation. It is also likely that as you do that you feel some of the same emotions that you felt last night. You may feel as upset and frustrated in your remembrance of the argument as you did during the argument itself. The memories of the event and the memories of the emotions that you felt last night can be attributed to the hippocampal system. The past emotions that you currently feel in the present (despite the fact that the argument is not currently happening) can be partially attributed to the amygdala system.

In this case, you have both implicit and explicit memories of the same event. Joseph LeDoux aptly remarked that the difference is that the hippocampal system creates "a memory of an emotion," while the amygdala system holds "an emotional memory."[11] These two types of memory can connect, as we've just seen, but this does not mean that they are fused together. If you are deeply upset by the loss of friendship, you may find yourself feeling nauseated when eating the same sort of meal that you had that night—*without* consciously thinking about the argument or the loss. Here the implicit memory is present but the explicit memory is absent. As time goes on, and you tell the story several more times, you might become able to tell the story without feeling any of the emotions that you previously felt. In this case, the explicit memory is present while the implicit memory fades.

The ability to connect implicit and explicit memories helps enable us to assert some measure of control in our emotional lives. It is what enables us to change our perspective or assign new meaning to a past event. The dynamic interaction between the hippocampal and amygdala systems and the rest of the brain is what makes this possible on the neurological level. Problems occur, however, when the hippocampus is not involved in the memory creation, which is thought to be the case in cases of trauma.

To understand how this can happen, it is necessary to briefly explore how explicit and implicit memories are formed in the brain. There are several regions of the brain that are thought to be responsible for responding to, organizing, and crystallizing an experience into a memory. The amygdala is thought to be responsible for the initial emotional response to the event, processing of basic social signals, and superficial assessment of meaning. The medial prefrontal cortex is thought to complete many higher cognitive functions, such as the integration of social signals. The brain stem controls the release of hormones to the central nervous system regulating things such as heart rate, temperature, and respiration based on signals that it receives from the amygdala. Finally, the hippocampus sorts the information sent by the amygdala and organizes it in relation to previous information. It is accordingly thought to be responsible for giving the subject a sense of her position in space and time, and, hence, to be critically involved, as noted above, in the subject's recall and relation to facts and autobiographical detail.

When an event occurs, the amygdala and the medial prefrontal cortex ascertain what is happening and what the body's response should be, sending this information along to the brain stem, which responds by activating the body accordingly through use of the hormone system. The information is then sent to the hippocampus that sorts it in relation to data that already exists. The job of the hippocampus in this regard can be likened to a filing system; the event occurs and the hippocampus organizes it, labels it, and files it away accordingly. When the event gets processed in these regions of the brain, it can become a distinct file that the subject can pull out and refer to in relation to the other events or files that the brain has already processed. Experiences that follow this particular course become explicit memories that the subject is able to bring to her attention and focus on, refer to, and think through. The formation of explicit memory *requires* the intervention of the hippocampus. When the hippocampus is not involved, which is sometimes the case in a traumatic event, the memories can still be stored by the mind, but they do not get encoded explicitly, and therefore *cannot* be brought forth as objects of attention.[12]

Neuroscientist Bessel van der Kolk defines a traumatic event as "an inescapably stressful event that overwhelms people's existing coping mechanisms."[13] When an event elicits an especially strong emotional response in the amygdala (i.e., one in which one feels significant threat), the neurobiological process focuses on adapting to that threat in the present. We can think of this as a kind of economics of blood flow. As a result, the hippocampal processes are overridden because forming higher-level autobiographical memories of the event is less important in the moment than survival.[14] Though this can become problematic, the process by which information bypasses certain sections of the brain is an evolutionarily adaptive one. When the subject is experiencing an event that is threatening, the amygdala sends information to the brain stem that the body is under attack. The brain stem responds by sending a signal to release stress hormones (norepinephrine, cortisol) that prepare the body to deal with that situation. Both of these hormones have functions that increase the chance of survival but decrease the likelihood of the creation of an explicit memory.[15]

Norepinephrine can be likened to a fire alarm; when it "goes off" or is released in the body, the senses are sharpened in order to perceive the specifics of the situation better, the heart rate and blood pressure are heightened to guarantee faster response time, and the body is prepared to respond to the threat quickly and effectively. In order to accomplish these enhancements, parts of the brain that are responsible for higher-level discernment, recognition, and cognition are temporarily diminished or shut down when norepinephrine is released into the system.[16] Cortisol aids in this process by re-prioritizing the bodily functions, redistributing energy in order to ensure effective and efficient response. Bodily functions that are not necessary in the moment are suppressed, so that the rest of the body can have the fuel that it needs to act. Some of the functions that get shut down are the immune system, the reproductive system, digestion, and the sensation of pain or fatigue.[17]

These are essential survival processes, and in the moment of a threat they are necessary. However, they are only beneficial in moderation. A small amount of norepinephrine is a good thing when it is necessary. If one is being attacked, for example, heightened senses and quicker bodily response time can be critical. However, when too much norepinephrine is released, or it is released chronically, the brain can become overwhelmed and freeze, or shut down in situations when it is not helpful or necessary. This process contributes to the experience of students who "choke" during an exam, or individuals who "freeze" when attempting to give a speech or performance in public.[18] Their bodies are so flooded with norepinephrine that the parts of their brain that are associated with language retrieval and movement are effectively offline. The same is true of cortisol; in moderation it can be life-saving, but in excess it can be seriously problematic. Chronic suppression of essential bodily processes when one is not *actually* under attack (as is the case in PTSD) can be destructive to the body. Chronically high cortisol can cause digestive disorders, sleep disorders, heart disease, immune system failure, and thinning of the bones, among other things.[19]

Perhaps the most important result of this increase in hormone levels for the present discussion of memory is the effect on the hippocampus. Increased hormone levels in the trauma response effectively shut the hippocampus down, as the organizing of data is less important than responding to that data in the moment. When the hippocampus is partially or completely shut off in order to promote more expedient processing in the brain, an autobiographical "memory" that the subject can *recognize* as a memory does not get fully formed. What *does* become encoded is an implicit memory or a set of somatic bodily responses, that is, increased heart rate, heightened senses, hyperarousal, and so on.

These bodily responses and emotions that are attached to the implicit memory can be triggered when the subject is reminded of the original event. When this occurs, she feels the emotions and goes through the bodily responses *as if she were experiencing the event all over again.* Claparède's patient illustrated this same result (though her brain injury was physiologically based and not caused by psychological trauma). For her, the memory of being pricked by a tack is implicit because she does not have access to the part of her brain that creates new explicit memories. When Claparède offers his hand to shake, the implicit memory brings forth an emotion of fear in the patient though she is not consciously aware of where the fear comes from. Something similar is happening in Shay's patient who mistakes a noise for grenade fire and his wife for an enemy combatant; because of the way that the memory was encoded in his brain, he *cannot distinguish* between the past experience of war and the present reality of being home and in bed. Though he may be rationally aware that he is not in Vietnam, past events come crashing in and take over in the form of implicit, somatic memory.

Part of the reason that this experience of memory can be so vivid and intrusive is due to the fact that an implicit, emotional memory overwhelms the ability to create and refer to an explicit conscious one. As van der Kolk explains,

> Neuroimaging research has shown that as people are reliving their trauma, the brain areas most involved in formal cognition are deactivated. So neuroscience research shows that when people are reliving, they cannot think rationally because the critical frontal lobe areas necessary for executive functioning go offline, and only the primitive fear, arousal, "my body's in danger," "I've got to run" parts of the brain light up.[20]

The implication here is that not only does the fear response inhibit the initial formation of the explicit memory, but that it continues to do so when the event gets relived through memory. This means that *each time* the event is triggered in the memory, the hippocampus is shut down all over again while the fear center is activated.[21]

Experiences of traumatic memories are vivid and intrusive because of the strength of connection created by conditioned fear response. When the amygdala responds to a threat by eliciting all of the processes just described, the neural connectivity of the brain changes. The brain learns, in effect, to respond to the threat based on the sensory environment that the threat occurred within.[22] When the environment or a remnant from the environment such as a smell, taste, or sound is replicated, the fear responses get re-activated.

If we think to the most common trope of the Vietnam veteran who hits the floor when a car backfires, we can now see why the implicit memory can be triggered by a singular sensory stimulus out of context. This causes the initial response from the traumatic event to recur, reigniting the somatic response executed in combat. The brain, as it were, "thinks" that it is under attack again and responds as if the threat is real, sparking a set of adaptive processes evolved for survival. What makes the formation of an explicit memory especially difficult in cases where the brain has come to have a conditioned fear response is the tendency of these responses to strengthen over time, rather than diminish. Neurological interventions to help victims heal from trauma attempt to reverse this phenomenon in the hope of two results, a diminished implicit memory and a strong and consciously available explicit memory.

Neurobiological research helps us to fill in the gaps behind traumatic symptoms and to understand biologically how traumatic events become imprinted or encoded in the brain, as well as why these memories are primarily implicit and somatic rather than explicit and conscious. It is worth noting here that the traumatic response occurs on a spectrum. In the most extreme cases, there might be no immediate access to the explicit memory of the event at all; there is only implicit affect and brain response. There are documented cases of patients who have no recollection of the traumatic event at all, but who still have significant psychological symptoms relating to the event. Van der Kolk describes working with trauma patients who have no memory of surviving the traumatic event, but find themselves inexplicably recreating the circumstances surrounding the event.[23] In one remarkable case, an individual who was a victim of a shooting but had no explicit memory of the event ended up reenacting an eerily similar scenario one year to the day later.[24] Extreme examples like this one, though they may not be consistent with every individual experience with trauma and traumatic memory, help illustrate the neurological basis of these symptoms of trauma.

In less extreme cases, which are much more common, explicit memory and implicit memory of the event can *both* exist in a dynamic relationship. This can be likened to the example described above, of experiencing an argument with a friend over dinner. In this case, you may feel the emotional response days and weeks later when you tell someone about the argument. Here the explicit memory is available, as you are able to focus consciously on the event and tell a story about it. The implicit memory is also available, which is why some of the feelings are elicited when you tell the story or think of it. Though in our everyday language, we might say that the argument was traumatic, the mere existence of the upsetting emotion is not enough to indication PTSD.

The difference between the emotional memory of this argument and the emotional memory of a traumatic event is that when the latter is triggered, the amygdala sets off a series of reactions that send the brain and body into fear response. Neurologically speaking, the implicit memory takes over the present moment and the result is the explicit memory becomes unavailable (if there was an explicit memory to begin with). In this case it is not necessarily true that the explicit memory does not *exist* (though this is possible), but that the explicit memory is not available because the implicit memory has overwhelmed the brain system.

Since the experience of traumatic memory repeatedly leads the brain down the fear response path, the implications of chronic PTSD are wide reaching and can be devastating. Implicit memories of the traumatic event are not limited to nightmares and private thought processes but can be triggered by many things and greatly diminish one's ability to interact with the world. Patients with PTSD have to negotiate constantly between the past and the present, and the results of constant hyperarousal can be both physically and psychologically damaging. Completing normal day-to-day tasks can be nearly impossible given the impact of traumatic memory on brain function.

SEEING TRAUMA IN THE BRAIN

Advancements in medical imaging technology have enabled scientists to gain an even clearer picture of these mechanisms in the brain. To give just one example, a fMRI study from 2009 shows just how a traumatic memory can impact one's ability to be fully present in the moment. The study, performed on veterans of the Iraq and Afghanistan wars who had been diagnosed with PTSD, examined the neural impact that trauma-related triggers had on basic cognitive processing. The hypothesis was that the nature of intrusion in traumatic memory negatively impacts cognitive processing for the victim, making it virtually impossible to complete goal-based tasks that require working memory.[25] The hypothesis turned out to be correct, as both the behavioral and fMRI results for the PTSD group showed that access to working memory was much lower than that of the control group as was subsequent ability to complete the goal-based task when facing combat-related triggers.[26]

In the PTSD group, three sections of the brain faced with a combat-trigger showed activity different from that of the control group. The amygdala (responsible for processing memory and emotional reactions), the ventrolateral prefrontal cortex (responsible for planning complex cognitive behavior), and the fusiform gyrus (responsible for face and body recognition, processing of color information, and other types of recognition) were all affected differently. The amygdala showed increased activity in the PTSD group, suggesting a much stronger emotional reaction to the trigger, while the ventrolateral prefrontal cortex showed decreased activity, suggesting a decreased ability to recognize forms and individuals and to access the short-term or working memory necessary to complete the task at hand. All of this means that when "triggered" by a traumatic memory, someone who has PTSD would be hard-pressed to complete any action that would require the use of working memory. Examples of tasks that require working memory could be carrying on a simple conversation, concentrating on a task at work, listening while your boss is giving you instructions, or taking notes during a lecture. Even more frustrating is that these deficiencies might only be present when one has been exposed to a traumatic trigger. One can see why veterans were often labeled weak or lazy (as discussed in chapter 1), as they might be able to complete a task without a problem one day and be incapable the next.

However, what the psychology and neuroscience show us is that when a traumatic memory is brought forward, the person traumatized can be—quite literally—taken out of the present. When a traumatized individual is reliving the traumatic memory, the working memory is inaccessible, leading to difficulties differentiating between the memory and the present, holding their environment in their mind, and recognizing familiar faces. We can see here quite starkly the way that the memories of the event continue to disrupt the mental structure of the individual.

The negative implications of these findings are both physiological and psychological. The failure of the mind to process a traumatic event in the way that it processes other events can lead to significant neurological injuries. It has been shown that patients who have been exposed to trauma and then become re-exposed through traumatic memory can come to have life-long difficulties with learning and memory. Studies have shown that trauma and traumatic memory can actually damage the brain, reducing the volume of the hippocampus. This reduced volume is associated with symptoms that mimic early dementia.[27] What is critical to recognize here is that it is not simply the initial experience of trauma that is destructive. The experience of having the memory continuously intrude on the present is *also* physically damaging. Reliving is retraumatizing.

The neuroscientific examination of trauma and traumatic memory provides substance to the structure provided by psychology. It does this by establishing a model for explaining why traumatic memories can be experienced as instances of reliving as well as illustrating the implications of being chronically re-exposed to the event. However, if we stop here, there is a danger of reducing the experience to simple biological explanations and simple diagnostic clusters. The reality is that the experience of trauma and post-trauma is irreducible to scientific explanation. What is still missing is the first-person lived experience. Understanding *what it is like* to experience the phenomena described here will not just simply add depth to the scientific explanations but will reframe our understanding of what is going on in traumatic memory in a critical way.

REFRAMING TRAUMATIC MEMORY WITH PHENOMENOLOGY

Russell Carr, who is the head of outpatient behavioral health at Walter Reed hospital, was deployed to Iraq in 2008 to treat difficult cases of soldiers who were exhibiting symptoms of PTSD while still in combat situations. This meant that he was tasked with developing a short-term treatment plan that could be used for soldiers who were suffering but needed to return to combat.

Carr quickly found that the standard interventions offered little help for these soldiers and began looking to alternative sources. He happened to have brought Robert Stolorow's book, *Trauma and Human Existence*, in which Stolorow turns to phenomenology to describe traumatic experience and its effects. Shortly after returning from Iraq, Carr wrote an article explaining how Stolorow's work on the phenomenology of trauma "fundamentally changed his understanding of trauma and its treatment."[28]

Carr argues that psychological interventions for combat trauma fail in part because they treat patients as a set of symptoms to fix, rather than as individuals who exist within a particular context. To put it in terms that Merleau-Ponty might use, the psychological viewpoint looked at the patients "from above," and thinks of them as "object[s] in general."[29] The phenomenological perspective provided by Stolorow allowed Carr to access his patients from a different viewpoint.

> Instead of seeing traumatized soldiers or Marines as having dysfunctional automatic thoughts, a shattered self, or a regressed ego, *I was beginning to feel that their experience of the world and themselves had been shattered.*[30]

This is the central contribution that phenomenology adds to the understanding of combat trauma—the idea that though there may be one specific incident of trauma, that the injury is much more global. Traumatic injury, viewed from a phenomenological perspective, is an injury that shatters one's entire blueprint of the world.

Carr was able to reach this understanding not through psychology or neuroscience alone but in bringing them together with the phenomenological lens. Phenomenology drew his attention to the importance of the patient's lived experience of the recent trauma and the ways in which that experience had altered the patient's beliefs about and experience within the world. Carr developed a successful short-term treatment plan based on the concepts laid out in *Trauma and Human Existence* and carried the book with him as he traveled between outposts and bases.

Merleau-Ponty's phenomenology adds another dimension to the discussion of trauma and traumatic memory.[31] One of the reasons that human beings cannot be reduced to scientific data is because to do so is to ignore what Merleau-Ponty would call their "being-in-the-world." Just as there is not a strict divide between the mind and the body, there is not a strict divide between a human being and the world that she exists within. Instead, she exists in dynamic interaction with the world, having before her a particular horizon, or phenomenal field that she engages with. In the broadest terms possible, the horizon is what is available to consciousness. However, there is a crucial caveat: what is perceived, what comprises the horizon, is shaped not just by objective truths in the external world, but also by meanings conveyed by and in pre-theoretical experience.

In order to understand what this means in general and then in regard to trauma, it is helpful to recall the constancy hypothesis and Merleau-Ponty's stance on it.[32] The constancy hypothesis is the claim that the inputs of consciousness have constancy to them in their correlation such that the same stimulus will consistently produce the same reaction. Merleau-Ponty rejects the constancy hypothesis. He argues that the reaction that a stimulus produces is determined not only by the stimulus, but also by the individual perceiving it. As he says, the perceptual apparatus is not just a "transmitter."[33] When we look at something, we don't simply *see* it. Rather, "it *awakens resonances* within our perceptive apparatus."[34] The resonances that are awoken are unique to each of us and to our horizons or phenomenal fields. This is a complicated (and beautiful) way of saying something rather simple. If a person begins struggling with insomnia, for example, it is likely that her perception of her bed will change as the meaning of it changes for her. What was once seen as a comfortable and warm place might start to actually look and feel like a prison cell. This shows that there is *not* constancy between the stimulus and the reaction that the stimulus produces. In other words, the things that we perceive are perceived *as* this or that, that is, as bearers of this or that meaning. They are perceived as meaningful in some way. What they are perceived as depends on the experiential horizon in which they appear.

This is relevant because things like the constancy hypothesis impact the way that we look at perception in general. In another example, Merleau-Ponty invites us to imagine a child who is attracted to the flame of a candle and touches it, burning herself. Merleau-Ponty points out that the child's perception of the candle changes from something attractive to something repulsive after this experience. We might be tempted to say that what is going on here is related to a kind of perceptual mistake related to knowledge of the objective world: the child did not know that the flame would burn her, so she misperceived it as something that she could grasp. This is, however, not accurate. It is *not* that the child had an incorrect perception, which has now been corrected since she has been exposed to the objective truth of the external world, but that her experience has colored her horizon such that the immediate perception of fire is now imbued with a different meaning.

To put it another way, vision changes when experiences are imbued with meaning—the resonances that it awakens were once attraction and are now fear or repulsion. Merleau-Ponty explains, "Vision is already inhabited by a meaning which gives it a function in the spectacle of the world and our existence."[35] In other words, it is incorrect to assume that we perceive things, and then reflect, and then establish meaning—it is more accurate to say that we perceive things *as* meaningful. It is these perceptions that are imbued with meaning based on our experience that colors the horizon.

There is much more that can be said about these basic ideas in Merleau-Ponty's phenomenology, and I expand on some of them in the following chapter. However, even this brief gloss on Merleau-Ponty's phenomenology of perception can be used to reframe the discussion of traumatic memory. The emphasis on meaning in perception helps to understand traumatic memory because it enables us to see that it is not simply that the trauma patient is misperceiving reality, but that *their perceptual world has been stamped with the trauma that they have sustained.*

To see this more vividly, we can take a look back at the examples from above. First, the veteran who cannot sleep through the night:

> I haven't spent a complete night in bed with my wife for at least ten years. I always end up on the sofa. It's safer for her. . . . After I couldn't work anymore . . . . I'd do this crazy [stuff] at night. I once threw her out of bed so hard it broke her shoulder. I thought there was an NVA potato-masher come in on us. Another night I thought she was [the enemy], and I had my hands around her throat before I woke up.[36]

To be sure, it is not objectively true that the veteran who hears grenade fire and then pushes his wife out of bed is actually under fire. However, it is not accurate to say that it is *false* either! The perception of gunfire and the chain of behavior that follows that perception are *very real* for the veteran. To reduce the experience of traumatic memory to an incorrect perception misses a vital part of the phenomenon as a *lived* experience.

The traumatic memories that this patient is dealing with are not just a psychological symptom, or a neurological problem in the brain. They are a sign that the traumatic events sustained have altered the fabric of his world, and that he perceives loud noises as threatening and his wife as the enemy. The issue is not that he is attempting to address a world that does not objectively exist and is therefore false. The problem is quite the opposite. The world in which he could be attacked at any moment *does* exist; it is his world. *He is addressing the world that the experience of trauma has created for him.* His horizon has become one of danger.

This reframing is vitally important because failing to understand the way that trauma has stamped the individual's world with a meaning that was not previously there risks reducing the experience to a kind of misperception. This reduction can lead to the conclusion that to fix the problem, the mistaken perception simply needs to be overridden. There are two problems with this conclusion. The first is that this approach does not work. When this veteran is in the midst of a traumatic flashback, it is not a matter of simply convincing him that he is wrong about objective reality. Even if that is helpful or necessary in the moment, it does not treat the underlying problem. The second problem is that to reduce traumatic memory to a symptom or a synaptic mistake is to ignore an essential part of what is going on for the patient. Again, the trauma *has altered the fabric of his horizon*; it is not just this particular instance of remembering that is a problem, but the very way that he perceives the world.

This is perhaps even more vivid in the second example from the section above.

> I am in the yard while playing the water hose upon the flagstones. Water stops running. After a while it begins again. Then the neighbor from whom I borrowed the hose comes out and reproaches me, finally swears at me, and then strikes me. Then all the neighbors come running out, and they chase me all over. Then I awaken in a sweat, feeling as though I had all the life pounded out of me.[37]

Again, it is not just this patient's dreams that are the problem; it is that his combat experience has shaped the entire world into an attack. His horizon has been colored in such a way that he sees neighbors and mundane gardening activities as dangerous. It is not just that he was under attack in the past, and that the past sometimes inconveniently peaks through into the present. It is that the past experience has shaped his perception so that *everything* is, at any moment, a potential attack. In both of these cases, Merleau-Ponty's phenomenology grants us access to a critical level of understanding that is missing from the psychological and neuroscientific accounts; namely, that these soldiers are not simply suffering from their traumatic memories, but as Carr explains, "that their experience of the world and themselves [has] been shattered."[38]

It is *vitally* important to understand that the phenomenological viewpoint is not at odds with the accounts in the sciences. This is why the viewpoint that gathers all of these perspectives together is best thought of as prismatic—if a prism is thought of as a transparent glass object whose distinct sides each offer a different viewpoint, through which other viewpoints are clarified and deepened. Consider how these perspectives work together.

The long-term effects of trauma and traumatic memory are not only destructive neurobiologically, as we have seen above. What the phenomenological viewpoint reveals is that the persistence of traumatic memory can chip away at the victim's sense of self, causing her to lose the feeling of authority over mental functions and over her body. Since the memory doesn't get encoded explicitly, or filed away, the subject cannot relate herself to that memory or recognize it as autobiographical. When the memory is relived the present morphs into the past and then back into the present without conscious awareness. Veterans perceive riverbanks in Maine *as* riverbanks in Vietnam—full of complex systems of tunnels built by the enemy soldier.[39] This is frustrating not because these things turn out to be false, but because the memory of them is so immediate, so vivid that there can be no distinction between the past and the present. As a result, victims become unable to trust their own perceptions in general. As one of Shay's patients describes, "Nothing is what it seems. That mountain there—maybe it wasn't there yesterday, and won't be there tomorrow. You get to the point where you're not even sure it is a mountain."[40]

This loss of trust in one's own perceptions is not limited to the objects that are or are not before one's immediate gaze in the moment, but also extends to the lens through which one navigates the world. We can see this in the patient above who says, "Nothing is what it seems." It is not simply the mind that is unsafe (as a Cartesian might conclude), but the *world*. In other words, after experiencing trauma and the subsequent irreality of a world in which one could be transported back to that awful moment at any moment, the knowledge that the world does not have an objective horizon that we can count on is inescapable. This forces a new perception of the world onto the individual. And *this* is perhaps the most profound injury that comes from trauma—the intractable loss of one's blueprint of the world.

Psychology provides the foundation for understanding traumatic symptomology and diagnostic paradigms, and neuroscience gives us a biological understanding of the nature of those symptoms as well as biologically based interventions. Phenomenology reveals that a key part of what has been injured is the experiential horizon through which human beings meaningfully navigate the world. What is injured in trauma is the victim's perception of the world—the injury is not that she perceives it incorrectly, but that it carries a terrible and powerful meaning that it didn't before.

Recall Claparède's pinprick experiment for example. Claparède might argue that his patient's response to the pin is entirely reducible to a synaptic occurrence on the brain level, but this isn't the whole story. The phenomenological perspective focuses on Claparède's patient as a whole being who exits within a certain horizon that has been shaped by her experience. Her automatic fear response makes sense not just because of what is going on in her brain, but because *we understand her to be an organism for whom bodily vulnerability and threat is an issue*. The pinprick is meaningful to her body, and so her body responds to the possible threat not simply because of reflex but because she is a being who is present in a particular horizon that is perceived *as* meaningful. Understanding the full extent of her experience, then, requires that we resist the temptation to only use reductionist accounts but eventually return to the "there-is" as Merleau-Ponty urges us. The reduction of this complicated human phenomenon to any one of these perspectives on its own is deficient. It does not suffice to simply register that the victim experiences nightmares and intrusive thoughts. Registering these experiences by no means adequately explains what this experience is like and what it means for the individual.

Instead of examining human experience at the mechanistic level of explanation, Merleau-Ponty urges us look to the "there is," the phenomenon as it occurs and what sorts of webs of human meaning and intentionality comprise it. A full account of trauma then would require a framework for understanding what it signifies to the victim of trauma, that is, what it means for her in her environment (as a being-in-the-world). The phenomenological account expands the horizon back out from Descartes's "I think, therefore I am," to "The world is not what I think, but what I live through."[41] By focusing on the lived experience of trauma, we are better equipped to understand and treat those parts of traumatic experience that seem to lie just outside the grasp of science. Again, it is not the case that the phenomenological perspective should replace the psychological or neuroscientific. Rather, given the complicated nature of human phenomena, the phenomenological perspective stands to enhance our understanding by adding an account of the meaning and impact of the lived experience to the discussion.

THE WARS CONTINUE

The prismatic approach to understanding trauma—one that includes the phenomenological perspective—is not just a way to approach the problem of combat PTSD, *it is the way we must approach this problem.* Only by looking from all possible vantage points can we come to understand the phenomenon as fully as possible.

At a hearing before the subcommittee on military personnel in 2013, Russell Carr gave a statement in which he said "the wars continue in our offices just like in every mental health clinic in the DOD. Almost everyone we see is suicidal."[42] During the hearing, Carr and others advocated for varied approaches to treatment because "one size is not going to fit all." Trauma—though there are certainly some generalizations that can be made about it—is as varied as the individuals who experience it. We need to expand our view of combat trauma and with it the treatment protocols that we use to treat it. This is not just about the successes of the treatment interventions, but about how we understand traumatic experience in the first place. A varied account enables us to better understand the phenomenon. This does not require that we dismiss diagnostic criteria, but that we integrate it with phenomenology.

Pursuing this prismatic account is our obligation. As Commander Carr concludes his statements in front of the subcommittee, "We cannot settle for success with only some of our service members and leave the rest behind allowing them to return to their hometowns as broken, tormented souls. The battle for our veterans' lives is one we cannot lose."[43]

If we want to stop losing, we need to keep track of what we have been missing. What we have been missing is the idea that what gets injured in combat trauma is one's blueprint of the world. But first, in the next chapter, I will reframe trauma in one more way—as an adaptive response borne of strength.

NOTES

1. Matthew Ratcliffe has also written about the way that phenomenology can enhance our understanding of traumatic memory in his wonderful book, *Real Hallucinations: Psychiatric Illness, Intentionality, and the Interpersonal World* (Cambridge, MA: The MIT Press, 2017).

2. It should be noted that though this chapter is centered on the experience of traumatic memory, occasional references will be made to symptoms outside of the B-cluster. This is because the symptoms from cluster B are not entirely distinct from symptoms from other clusters. The symptoms discussed in this chapter are all related in some way to the re-experiencing of traumatic event through memory.

3. American Psychiatric Association, *Diagnostic and Statistical Manual of Mental Disorders*, vol. 5 (Washington, DC: American Psychiatric Association Press, 2013), 265–290. The first three symptoms listed here are directly concerned with memories that are represented in consciousness. The last two have to do with the experience of having a sense memory triggered by an external stimulus. This distinction will be made clear in section 2.2, which discusses the way that memories are coded in the brain, and explains the difference between explicit (conscious) and implicit (somatic, bodied) memories.

4. Bessel van Der Kolk, Alexander McFarlane, and Lars Weisæth, *Traumatic Stress: The Effects of Overwhelming Experience on Mind, Body, and Society* (New York: Guilford, 1996), 280.

5. Jonathan Shay, *Achilles in Vietnam: Combat Trauma and the Undoing of Character* (New York: Simon & Schuster, 1995), xvii.

6. Shay, *Achilles in Vietnam,* 172.

7. Abram Kardiner, *Traumatic Neuroses of War* (Mansfield, CT: Martino Publishing, 2012), 91.

8. There are many sources that provide much more detailed explanations of the neuroscience than can be spelled out here. Many of them are accessible to those who have no background in neuroscience. See, for example: Joseph LeDoux, "Emotional Memory Systems in the Brain," *Behavioral Brain Research* 58 (1993): 69–79; Bessel A. van der Kolk, "Trauma and Memory," *Psychiatry and Clinical Neurosciences* 52 (1998): 52–64; Bessel A. van der Kolk, *The Body Keeps the Score: Brain, Mind, and Body in the Healing of Trauma* (New York: Viking, 2014), esp. pp. 51–105 & 171–202. Stephen Porges's work on the polyvagal theory is also helpful here. See

Stephen Porges, "Orienting in a Defensive World: Mammalian Modifications of Our Evolutionary Heritage. A Polyvagal Theory," *Psychophysiology* 32 (1995): 301–318. This section will provide a simplified account of current work on memory within neuroscience. The views presented here are consistent with the current studies and commonly held theories in the field. There are of course debates and nuances within neuroscience regarding memory, and many more parts of the brain involved with memory creation and maintenance. These more detailed considerations will not be taken up here since the goal in the present context is to understand traumatic memory and distinguish between regular memories and traumatic memories, while providing an overview of the most prevalent scientific account of traumatic memory.

9. This may require some effort sometimes, but the memory is at least potentially available for recollection in the case of explicit memory.

10. LeDoux, *The Emotional Brain*, 180–182.

11. Ibid., 182.

12. Ibid., 179–224. As we saw above, implicit memories are not necessarily negative. When someone learns to play the piano, or drive, this memory still gets encoded in the mind. Over time, these memories get encoded implicitly rather than explicitly. When people refer to a musician's ability to play without thinking as "muscle memory," or the ability one has to drive to work "without thinking," these are examples of implicit memory at work. They shape the function of the individual, but are not brought to attention. In fact, since the hippocampus is thought to develop at age two, anything learned in the first year of life (which typically includes walking and talking at very basic levels) is encoded as implicit memory that is called upon for the rest of one's life. We cannot, however, remember facts or retain any sense of autobiographical memory until the hippocampus is developed.

13. van der Kolk, McFarlane, and Weisæth, *Traumatic Stress*, 279.

14. LeDoux, "Emotion Circuits in the Brain," 155–184.

15. J. Douglas Bremner, "Does Stress Damage the Brain? Understanding Trauma-Related Disorders from a Mind-Body Perspective," *Directions in Psychiatry* (2004): 167–176; J. D. Bremner, et al., "Deficits in Short-term Memory in Posttraumatic Stress Disorder," *American Journal of Psychiatry* 150, no. 7 (1993): 1015–1019; J. D. Bremner, et al., "Cortisol Response to a Cognitive Stress Challenge in Posttraumatic Stress Disorder (PTSD) Related to Childhood Abuse," *Psychoneuroendocrinology* 28 (2003): 733–750.

16. See, for example: J. Douglas Bremner, "Traumatic Stress: Effects on the Brain," *Dialogues in Clinical Neuroscience* 8 (2006): 445–461; Lisa Shin, et al., "Regional Cerebral Blood Flow During Script-driven Imagery in Childhood Sexual Abuse-Related PTSD: A PET Investigation," *American Journal of Psychiatry* 156 (1999): 575–584; E. D. Abercrombie and B. L. Jacobs, "Single-unit Response of Noradrenergic Neurons in the Locus Coeruleus of Freely Moving Cats. II. Adaptation to Chronically Presented Stressful Stimuli," *Journal of Neuroscience* 7 (1987): 2844–2848.

17. See, for example, R. M. Sapolsky, "Why Stress is Bad for Your Brain," *Science* 273, no. 5276 (1996): 749–750; R. M. Sapolsky, et al., "Hippocampal Damage Associated With Prolonged Glucocoricoid Exposure in Primates," *Journal of*

Neuroscience 10 (1990): 2897–2902; J. D. Bremner, et al., "Elevated CSF Corticotropin-releasing Factor Concentrations in Posttraumatic Stress Disorder," *American Journal of Psychiatry* 154 (1997): 624–629; T. V. Gurvits, et al., "Magnetic Resonance Imaging Study of Hippocampal Volume in Chronic Combat-Related Posttraumatic Stress Disorder," *Biological Psychiatry* 40 (1996): 192–199.

18. Bremner, "Does Stress Damage the Brain," 167–176.

19. Ibid.

20. Bessel van Der Kolk and Lisa M. Najavits, "Interview: What is PTSD Really? Surprises, Twists of History, and the Politics of Diagnosis and Treatment," *Journal of Clinical Psychology: In Session* 69, no. 5 (2013): 516–522.

21. For a more in depth treatment of the areas of the brain involved in traumatic memory, see J. W. Hopper, et al., "Neural Correlates of Reexperiencing, Avoidance, and Dissociation in PTSD: Symptom Dimensions and Emotion Dysregulation in Responses to Script-Driven Trauma Imagery," *Journal of Traumatic Stress* 20, no. 5 (2007): 713–725.

22. LeDoux, "Emotion Circuits in the Brain," 175.

23. van der Kolk, McFarlane, and Weisæth, *Traumatic Stress*, 283.

24. Ibid.

25. Working memory is the ability to hold the immediate environment in the mind and relate to it in reference to other memory. LeDoux defines it as "a serially organized mental workspace where things can be compared and contrasted and mentally manipulated" (LeDoux, "Emotion Circuits in the Brain," 175).

26. Specifically, the fMRI data suggests that in the presence of combat-related distractors, activity in the brain associated with working memory was disrupted while activity in the brain associated with emotion was enhanced. See R. A. Morey, et al., "The Role of Trauma-Related Distractors on Neural Systems for Working Memory and Emotion Processing," *Journal of Psychiatric Research* 43, no. 8 (2009): 807–817.

27. See, for example, C. G. Schmahl, et al., "Magnetic Resonance Imaging of Hippocampal and Amygdala Volume in Women with Childhood Abuse and Borderline Personality Disorder," *Psychiatry Research: Neuroimaging* 1222 (2003): 193–198; D. B. Baker, et al., "Serial CSF Corticotropin-releasing Hormone Levels and Adrenocortical Activity in Combat Veterans With Posttraumatic Stress Disorder," *American Journal of Psychiatry* 156 (1999): 585–588; J. D. Bremner, et al., "MRI-based Measurement of Hippocampal Volume in Posttraumatic Stress Disorder Related to Childhood Physical and Sexual Abuse: A Preliminary Report," *Biological Psychiatry* 41 (1997): 23–32.

28. Russell Carr, "Combat and Human Existence: Toward an Intersubjective Approach to Combat-Related PTSD," *Psychoanalytic Psychology* (June 2011): 1–27.

29. Merleau-Ponty, "Eye and Mind," 160.

30. Carr, "Combat and Human Existence," 3, emphasis added.

31. Thomas Fuchs also uses Merleau-Ponty's work in order to examine the way that traumatic memory is an embodied experience. See, for example, Thomas Fuchs, "Body Memory and the Unconscious," *Phaenomenologica* 199 (2012): 69–82.

32. Merleau-Ponty, *Phenomenology of Perception*, 30.

33. Ibid., 10.
34. Maurice Merleau-Ponty, *In Praise of Philosophy and Other Essays*, trans. James M. Edie, John Wild, and John O'Neill (Evanston, IL: Northwestern University Press, 1988), 17.
35. Merleau-Ponty, *Phenomenology of Perception*, 52.
36. Shay, *Achilles in Vietnam*, xvii.
37. Kardiner, *Traumatic Neuroses of War*, 91.
38. Carr, "Combat and Human Existence," 3.
39. Shay, *Achilles in Vietnam*, 170.
40. Ibid.
41. Merleau-Ponty, *Phenomenology of Perception*, xviii.
42. Government of United States, "Hearing before the Subcommittee on Military Personnel of the Committee on Armed Services," One Hundred Thirteenth Congress, First Session, April 10, 2013. https://www.gpo.gov/fdsys/pkg/CHRG-113hhrg80753/pdf/CHRG-113hhrg80753.pdf.
43. Ibid.

Chapter 3

Rethinking the Roots of Trauma

A Phenomenology of Adaptation

The roots of the study of combat trauma begin in the United States with Abram Kardiner. Kardiner was an anthropologist and a psychoanalyst in New York in the 1920s and 1930s. He worked in a veterans' hospital in the Bronx, and his contributions to the field of trauma studies were significant. Much of the reason that the diagnostic criteria is structured the way it is in the DSM is because of Kardiner. He is most famous for his work *The Traumatic Neuroses of War* (1941), in which he speculated that traumatic symptoms post combat are a result of a disruption in one's ability to adapt. Traumatic symptoms arise when "an adaptation is injured, spoiled, disorganized, or shattered."[1] He goes on to explain that in most of our dealings, we can adapt to whatever we are facing. In trauma, we are met with an external stimulus that leaves us unable to "adjust to, sidestep, or otherwise master the stimulus."[2]

Though we may have imported much of Kardiner's work into the current diagnostic criteria for PTSD, this idea that PTSD originates in a disruption of one's typical adaptive mechanisms has dropped out of our understanding. Whether we are looking at it as a disease, sickness, or an illness, we see it as a *disorder*, a failure to function, a sign of weakness, something to be ashamed of. This is especially salient in situations in which veterans are compared to one another. The logic goes like this—veteran X experienced the same things as veteran Y, but only veteran X has PTSD, so there must have already been something wrong with veteran X. This logic is not only deeply flawed in the sense that it operates on the false assumption that we all experience the world in the exact same way, but it also gets in the way of successfully treating veterans in two ways. First, it incorrectly assumes that the origin of the disorder lies elsewhere—not within the traumatic experience but in childhood, or a previously undiscovered chemical imbalance. This, after all, would be an easy way to explain the incongruence. If X and

Y were both exposed to the same stressor, armed with the same coping skills, X's development of PTSD cannot be explained by the stressor alone. Second, it operates on the idea that trauma is a sign of weakness and disorder all the way to its roots. The underlying assumption here is that there is already something wrong with X, and that combat merely pushed him over the edge. In either case, the development of PTSD seems to be the fault of the sufferer. The veteran either has PTSD because they have past issues (other traumas or psychological issues) that they have not dealt with, or because they are weak.

While it is the case that *some* people who develop PTSD post combat have trauma in their pasts or undiscovered mental illness, this is *certainly* not true for all. To define PTSD this way is to stigmatize and shame the sufferer—creating a situation in which the very definition of PTSD itself becomes a barrier to care.

In this chapter, I will continue to develop a phenomenological and prismatic account of trauma with an eye on these ideas of injury and adaptation and how they might reframe our definition of combat trauma. If PTSD is at its roots an injury in one's ability to adapt—and as I will argue one that arises out of survival instinct—we can see that PTSD is *not* the fault of the survivor nor is it the result of weakness. Rather, it is evidence of an inherent strength and a vital urge to survive.

EMBODIMENT AND TRAUMATIC INJURY

In the previous chapter, we saw that Merleau-Ponty's phenomenology offers a way of reframing the discussion of traumatic memory by returning to the "there-is"—or the lived experience—of the trauma. Rather than the scientific gaze, which looks on from above, a phenomenology of trauma begins with the experience of trauma and traumatic memory as an experience that is lived through by a particular individual. It aims at understanding what it is like for the victim and revealing the way that trauma can color the victim's horizon. When added to the perspectives of neuroscience and psychology, the phenomenological stance provides a new depth to our understanding of traumatic memory.

Beyond reframing the discussion of traumatic memory specifically, phenomenology can also provide a more thorough account of traumatic injury in general. This section further explores the phenomenology of trauma by focusing on the role of the embodied subject in the experience of traumatic injury. By demonstrating that a crucial part of what has been injured is the victim's way of being in and communicating with the world, this focus yields a more thorough understanding of traumatic injury.

With a view to avoiding mistakes made by reductionist accounts, Merleau-Ponty's phenomenology focuses on human life as it is lived. Doing so demands seeing an individual as embodied rather than as a disembodied consciousness (the Cartesian *cogito*). It is a chief aim of the *Phenomenology of Perception* to show the ways in which human phenomena defy reduction, and therefore can only be fully understood when the embodied individual *and* her horizon are taken into account. As we saw in the previous chapter, when Merleau-Ponty gives the example of the child who gets burned by the flame of a candle and then comes to perceive fire as dangerous, it is revealed that perceptions are imbued with meaning based on the experience of a bodied being that engages with the world. In other words, instead of a dualistic understanding of the world in which there is a separation between the mind and body, the body plays a fundamental role in consciousness. The mind and body are synthesized in his view, rather than divided, as an embodied experience shapes and is shaped the horizon.

In order to illustrate that human behavior cannot be reduced to simple causal explanations, Merleau-Ponty presents examples of cases that resist this kind reduction in the *Phenomenology of Perception*. In addition to frequently involving patients who have suffered trauma, these examples present pathologies that challenge prevailing scientific explanation. In this way, Merleau-Ponty uses the paradigms of illness and injury to make and then strengthen his claims about the nature of embodiment.

Through his analysis of such cases, Merleau-Ponty also shows the way in which the phenomenological perspective can enhance our understanding of injury. Merleau-Ponty concentrates his analysis most frequently on the fascinating case of Johann Schneider, a combat veteran who sustained injuries from mine-splinters in World War I.[3] Merleau-Ponty discusses several different aspects of Schneider's condition in order to point out how Schneider's symptoms defy simple physiological or psychological explanation. As a Merleau-Ponty scholar remarks, "Schneider led Merleau-Ponty to reconceive the body in terms that were neither exclusively mechanistic nor entirely intentional but somehow incorporating both."[4] Before moving to Merleau-Ponty's analysis of Schneider, it is helpful to further give a more detailed examination of embodiment in phenomenology and how it contributes to our understanding of human existence.

EMBODIMENT REVISITED

Embodied beings are said to be beings-in-the-world. Being human necessarily entails existing within a certain physical context or situation. As Merleau-Ponty explains, being-in-the-world "anchors the subject to a certain 'environment.'"[5] What this means is that human existence is not an objective and untethered phenomenon that can be sectioned off and examined in pieces, but instead is situational, contextual, and therefore *must* be considered as such. Experience *cannot* and does not occur independent of a situation. Nor is it the case that embodied beings experience the objective, external world from a distance. Rather, embodied existence always involves a kind of dynamic interaction with the world, and it is shaped both by the meaningful horizon created by past experience (as we saw in the last chapter), and also by the ways in which the body engages with the world in the moment. Merleau-Ponty explains further:

> When we say that an animal exists, that it has a world, or that it belongs to a world, we do not mean that it has a perception or objective consciousness of that world. The situation . . . is experienced as an "open" situation, and "requires" the animal's movements, just as the first notes of a melody require a certain kind of resolution, without its being known in itself.[6]

A beautiful way of saying something quite simple: the boundaries between self and world are not as distinct as they might appear. We do not perceive and interact with the world in slices, our consciousness (which includes the body) projects forward into the future, anticipating the melody as we listen. As he says, "There is no inner man, man is in the world, and only in the world does he know himself."[7] Existing means existing in the world, which necessarily entails a kind of belonging to it, engaging with it; and this belonging to and engaging with is necessarily bodied.

Recall Claparède's patient from the previous chapter. If we are to assume that a human being has an objective consciousness of the world that shapes her behavior, then it *must* be the case that Claparède's patient refuses to shake his hand because she is consciously aware of the tack. However, as a result of her injuries, this *cannot* be the case. She flinches when Claparède reaches to shake her hand, not because she has conscious awareness of the outside world, but because she exists within a certain situation that is meaningful for her as an *embodied being*. To make use of Merleau-Ponty's musical metaphor from the passage above, the presence of Claparède represented to her a dangerous sounding melody, which calls for a cautious response. Claparède's patient does not exist as a body or as a mind in the objective world, but as an *embodied being-in-the-world*. The contours of her experience are shaped both by her past and by numerous variables presented to her body in the present moment.

To give another example, the perspective of the reader is shaped by her body as she reads. The particular issues that her body is currently facing are a critical part of her current situation and therefore shape her consciousness in important ways. Her frame of reference will shift based on where her body is, how it feels, and what it needs. The experience of reading will be different if she is comfortably sitting in her study, versus standing on the street in a snowstorm waiting for a bus, or sitting on an airplane during turbulence, for example. It will be different if she is reading while tired, or hungry, or feeling anxious after an argument with a friend. To experience *anything* in the world is to experience it from a particular standpoint or within a particular situation. To attempt to understand the situation by separating it from the behavior that emerges is a mistake. When you dissect a frog in eighth grade biology class, you are not left with a vibrant, leaping, ribbiting frog with a beating heart. You are left with cold, grayish, rubbery pieces of frog that smell of formaldehyde, which makes everyone nauseous. The distinction between the two is important, and what we can learn from the dissected frog—though important—is *limited.* It lacks the vital embeddedness of embodied life.

Another mistake often made is the assumption that experience is a purely passive phenomenon. We do not passively take in the external world; we exist within it, interact with it and are engaged with it *by virtue* of our embodiment. I do not simply stand on the sand and passively see the sea, my toes are *in* the sand, and I perceive the sea as meaningful in some way. It is representative of many things: wildness, the feeling of openness, a certain kind of exciting terror. I do not simply *see* the sea, I engage with it. Were my body to change and I were to become unable to swim, the sight of the ocean might invoke different feelings (e.g., nostalgia from when I could swim, fear at being close to the water, and unable to swim). The point is that the boundaries between the embodied individual and her environment are not clear and distinct, but bleed together in the experience itself. So, if a robust understanding of behavior is the goal, it is necessary to take into account how the individual exists and experiences within her particular context and situation. Further, it is important to recognize the way that the context and situation and the individual's place within it is ever shifting.

This theory of embodiment shows the limitations inherent in attempting to generalize embodied behavior in the way that science often attempts. If Merleau-Ponty is correct about experience, *any* attempt to separate behavior from its embodied context will always yield a somewhat distorted view. M. C. Dillon explains that for Merleau-Ponty "the functioning of the lived body resists comprehension as long as its mind is conceived as disjunct from its flesh and the spheres of immanence and transcendence are regarded as mutually exclusive."[8] In other words, the lived body can *only* be clearly understood when it is taken as a unity that is always embedded within a particular environment.

To illustrate this point, Merleau-Ponty discusses the ways in which even predictable bodily response to stimuli *always* reveals a being-in-the-world, embodiment within a particular environment. If two people are asked to draw a circle on a blackboard with a piece of chalk, they might execute the same action in two different ways. One might draw a circle with her arm extended, the other with her arm bent at the elbow.[9] What this suggests is that even essentially predictable behavior admits to variety, and therefore behavior is only predictable *to a certain extent.*[10]

To be in the world, then, is not just to be an intact subject who passively perceives the external world. To be in the world is to perceive things *as* meaningful. It is to exist *as* a body entangled within a particular situation and interacting with it. To fully understand *any* embodied experience, then, one must examine the particularities of it within the embodied context in which it occurs. If this is true of human experience in general, it is surely true of the experience of traumatic injury. This can be seen more vividly in Merleau-Ponty's analysis of Schneider.

THE CASE OF SCHNEIDER

In general, Schneider's injuries (sustained in combat) seem to reveal the way that human existence is embodied, and to underscore that there are dimensions of human experience that are irreducible to the causal accounts given by science.[11] At several points in the *Phenomenology of Perception*, Merleau-Ponty points out the limitations of scientific explanation to grasp the extent and nature of Schneider's symptoms. These symptoms can *only* be understood, he argues, by moving to the phenomenological perspective, the one that returns to the "there-is" instead of looking on from above. Merleau-Ponty's interest is not limited to Schneider's particular case, but rather what this case can show us about human existence in general. The analysis of Schneider acts as a paradigm for embodiment by revealing the ways in which any attempt to catalogue and generalize symptoms of traumatic injury encounters limitations when they do not take into account what it means to be in the world. Further, the analysis of Schneider helps us isolate what it means to be embodied *and* injured. I will examine two central symptoms that Schneider dealt with and how Merleau-Ponty re-thinks them from a phenomenological perspective.

One of the symptoms that interested Merleau-Ponty was what he called Schneider's "sexual inertia."[12] After the war, Schneider became impotent, but the source of his dysfunction proved difficult to pinpoint. Schneider was not biologically impotent, but was at the same time incapable of seeking out or engaging in sexual activity. In other words, as a biological organism, Schneider was fully capable of sexual activity, but as a human being he was not.[13] Merleau-Ponty describes the symptoms as follows:

> Obscene pictures, conversations on sexual topics, the sight of a body do not arouse desire in him. The patient hardly ever kisses, and the kiss for him has no value as sexual stimulation. Reactions are strictly local and do not begin to occur without contact. If the prelude is interrupted at this stage, there is no attempt to pursue the sexual cycle. In the sexual act intromission is never spontaneous. If orgasm occurs first in the partner and she moves away, the half-fulfilled desire vanishes. *At every stage it is as if the subject did not know what is to be done.*[14]

What is somewhat baffling about Schneider's symptoms here is that they do not align with scientific explanations of sexuality. A scientific account—certainly one from 1945, but even one from today—might postulate that sexual desire is a biological and physiological function wherein visual or tactile stimuli set off a series of bodily and synaptic events that lead to sexual desire, impulse and eventually activity. On this account, sexual dysfunction can be explained either by a physical or psychological injury that thwarts the series of events and thus prevents the completion of the cycle. Schneider's symptoms challenge this model of sexuality because he has no sexual impulse *despite the fact that these areas in his brain and body are apparently intact and functioning.*[15] Merleau-Ponty points out that it is not the case that Schneider can no longer see sexual images, or feel erotic touch, but that he can no longer experience those images or tactile experiences *as* sexual. They no longer carry sexual value for him. He is incapable of sexual activity not because of some traceable malfunction in his body or in his brain, but because sex no longer holds *meaning* for him.[16]

In other words, what has been injured is Schneider's ability to adapt to a sexual situation, to decipher sexual meaning, or to attach sexual value to anything in his horizon. Rather than seeking a physiological or intentional source to explain his sexual behavior, Merleau-Ponty locates the problem in Schneider's being-in-the-world. As Merleau-Ponty explains, Schneider's problem is that "he does not live" the situation, he "is not caught up in it."[17] The implication here is that in order to "live into" a sexual encounter, Schneider must be able to experience a situation such that the object of his consciousness is himself in a (future) situation that is imbued with sexual meaning. Schneider cannot do this; his life has lost its sexual meaning because he can no longer imbue his experience with it. His perceptions have lost their "erotic structure, both spatially and temporally" because he has lost the "power of projecting before himself a sexual world."[18] The same is true for pointing to his ankle—he has lost his ability to project his body schema forward enough to take his body as an object to be grasped or pointed to. This does not mean, however, that his body does not exist for him. When it itches, Schneider does not need to consciously project his body forward into the future, he simply needs to scratch. The reason that Schneider's symptoms cannot be explained by psychology or biology alone is because the symptoms have more to do with the way that Schneider exists within and engages with the world and less to do with some locatable, reducible biological or psychological dysfunction.

Schneider's sexuality is especially relevant because for Merleau-Ponty, understanding the body in its sexual being "brings to light the birth of being for us."[19] If an investigation of perception can uncover the perceiver's embodied relationship with her world, an investigation of sexuality can illuminate the embodied relationship that holds between individuals. Merleau-Ponty argues that an examination of sexuality is essential because it can help us "come to understand better how things and beings can exist in general."[20] Schneider's sexuality is relevant because it shows sexuality in *general* to be paradigmatic of the embodied being-in-the-world.

Sexuality is, as Merleau-Ponty says, "one more form of original intentionality. . . . Sexuality is not an autonomous cycle. It has internal links with the whole active and cognitive being."[21] In other words, sexuality *shows* human experience and existence to be necessarily embodied. It is an example that illustrates the way in which experience is always presented within a context and cannot be reduced to its singular properties and effects. The fact that sexuality cannot be reduced to a definition of response (or failure to respond) to internal or external stimuli reveals the way in which human life is irreducible to mind or body, and rather emerges through the interplay between the two. In Merleau-Ponty's words, "The life of the body, or the flesh, and the life of the psyche are involved in a relationship of reciprocal expression."[22] Flesh and psyche cannot be torn apart, they reflect each other.

The examination of Schneider's sexual inertia, then, becomes a conduit for Merleau-Ponty's argument that human behavior in general cannot be reduced to simple scientific explanation. What Schneider illustrates in this particular case is that sexuality in general cannot be understood as automatic biological responses to stimuli. If sexuality is taken to *simply* be a response to stimuli and nothing more, a crucial step is missing. An essential part of sexuality involves the way that a person engages with the world—specifically, a capacity to project herself into a meaningful sexual situation. The viewpoint of phenomenology can better understand what is happening in this case because it examines the experience holistically. Through the exploration of Schneider's sexual inertia, Merleau-Ponty seeks to describe human sexuality in general (and by extension human behavior in general) as an embodied phenomenon that defies atomistic, reductionist explanation. The analysis of Schneider's sexual dysfunction then acts as an illustration of one of the ways in which human beings are embodied.

What Schneider's sexual inertia suggests is that a full understanding of *any* injury requires looking beyond the generalizable symptoms and into the experience of the patient in her world.[23] We cannot gain a full understanding of what is going on by simply tracing back to what is failing to occur (or over-occurring) in the mind or the body. Rather, a crucial part of understanding what has been injured involves taking into account Schneider as an embodied being-in-the-world who exists within a particular situation. Similar to the victim described in chapter 2 who comes to perceive the world *as* dangerous in light of his traumatic experience, Schneider isn't just incapable of sexual intercourse; Schneider's world has been altered in that his ability to perceive a situation *as* sexual has been extinguished. This reframing may seem like it rests on a small distinction. However, when this method is applied to our understanding of traumatic injury, it allows us to reframe and perhaps even redefine traumatic injury entirely.

To see this more clearly, consider another symptom that is analyzed by Merleau-Ponty, which is Schneider's aphasia, a language disorder marked by disturbances in comprehension or expression of language. Again using Schneider's specific symptoms to make more general claims about human beings, Merleau-Ponty argues that speech is an embodied, dynamic process.

A reductionist account might hold that speech acts are a result of a series of synaptic connections in the brain. Though it is certainly true that brain synapses play an essential role in language and communication, to assume that speech acts are a result of these connections in the brain and nothing more is to obscure key aspects of the phenomena. Speech is undeniably partially a biological process involving synapses in the brain. However, it is *also* an act whereby a subject expresses herself. Merleau-Ponty argues that to understand speech as a mere function in the brain in which subjects learn to attach words to mental images is to strip speech of its power to express meaning. Language is another method through which the embodied subject exists within and communicates with the world. As Merleau-Ponty explains,

> *The word, far from being the mere sign of objects and meanings, inhabits things* and is the vehicle of meanings. Thus speech, in the speaker, does not translate ready-made thought, but accomplishes it.[24]

Words *inhabit* things. Though it is tempting to dissect language from objects, the word that we associate with an object is *not* separate from our perception of the object. Merleau-Ponty argues that when someone opens her mouth and speaks, it is not necessarily the case that she has fully formulated a coherent thought and is now translating it from her brain to the world. Rather, thinking and speaking *coexist*. When we see a chair, for example, we do not perform a linear set of actions in which the object of our perception is subsumed under the concept "chair" and only then can be uttered. Rather, the speech act emerges from a connection between perception, meaning, and articulation. As Merleau-Ponty explains, words are "behind me, like things behind my back, or like the city's horizon around my house, I reckon with them or rely on them, but without having any 'verbal image.'"[25] It is not the case, then, that words float around in the mind waiting to be attached to concepts. Rather, we exist within horizons, situations, or contexts, and speech emerges through our experience.

This difficult concept actually becomes easier to understand when we add the body back in. The way that we articulate our experience is related to the way that our bodies engage with the world. Dreyfus gives a helpful example of how our experience as embodied beings creates an environment in which the word inhabits the object. As he says,

> Because we have the sort of bodies that get tired and that bend backwards at the knees, chairs can show up to us—but not flamingos, say—as affording sitting. But chairs can only solicit sitting once we have learned to sit. Finally, only because we Western Europeans are brought up in a culture where one sits on chairs do they solicit us to sit on them. Chairs would not solicit sitting in traditional Japan.[26]

Though Dreyfus is making a point about embodiment, his point also applies to the way that language relates to the world. If words inhabit things, what the word inhabits will differ depending on the context in which it appears. In traditional Japan, the word "chair" would not necessarily refer to the same object that it would refer to in the United States (translation issues aside). This matters. For thought, speech, meaning, and the way that these three things come together as we engage with the world around us. A native Japanese speaker who grew up in traditional Japan could be taught the English word "chair." That very same person might still be baffled if asked to sit down in one. What we say and what we mean are both inexorably connected to how we engage in the world as bodied beings.

In Merleau-Ponty's account, then, speech is not *just* a biological process and therefore cannot be dissected so easily. It is at once embodied and contextual, shaped by the ways in which the subject engages with the world and articulates her experience of it. Merleau-Ponty wants to jettison the reductionist explanation of speech in favor of one that defines speech as an act by which we engage with the world.

Merleau-Ponty argues that the complex relationship between thought and speech can be illustrated by examining Schneider's aphasia, which has seemingly left him incapable of using or understanding certain words. If the reductionist view of speech that Merleau-Ponty is trying to disprove were correct, then a patient suffering from aphasia would *completely* lose the word that matched up with the mental image. What is peculiar about aphasia, however, is that one may recognize a specific word in one situation but not in another.

When speaking about Schneider's aphasia, Merleau-Ponty makes it clear that Schneider has not so much lost a capacity as he has lost an ability to put that capacity into use in some situations. As Merleau-Ponty explains, "What the patient has lost, and what the normal person possesses, is not a certain stock of words, but *a certain way of using them.*"[27] In other words, it is not as if there is a set of index cards that went missing when Schneider was injured. It is not that the words are somehow gone. The problem lies in Schneider's capacity to use the word to signify a particular meaning. Further, just because this symptom is rooted in speech, this does not mean that the body is not involved. Instead, as Merleau-Ponty explains, language *is* bodied.

> A contraction of the throat, a sibilant emission of air between the tongue and teeth, a certain way of bringing the *body into play* [which] suddenly allows itself to be invested with figurative significance which is conveyed outside of us.[28]

Language does not exist without bodies that speak it or gesture it. Again, as was the case regarding his sexuality, the injury pertains to the way that Schneider exists in the world as an embodied being and therefore cannot be explained through scientific reduction.

More contemporary studies on language and speech have corroborated Merleau-Ponty's explanation of aphasia. For example, studies have shown that individuals can still recognize words from which whole phonemes are missing.[29] In one study, the experimenters presented participants with sentences from which whole phonemes have been removed. Not only could the participants understand the sentence, *they did not even realize the phonemes were missing*. However, when given these words (with the phonemes removed) in isolation, participants were unable to understand the word and all of them realized the phonemes were missing.[30]

On the reductionist account of vision and language, these situations should be impossible. If understanding speech depended merely on the recording of stimuli, then the participants should have both been unable to understand the sentences *and* should have noticed the phonemes missing (as they did when given words without context).[31] However, if we understand speech to be meaningful only in an embodied and situational context, we can see how the horizons of meaning project into the future during speech and help us fill in the missing sounds because of the meanings given by the context of these words.[32] As Merleau-Ponty says, "We refute both intellectualism and empiricism by simply saying that *the word has a meaning.*"[33] Rather than understanding language as expressing thoughts, we are to understand language as a way in which we exist in and interact with the world. Language is a way that we express ourselves, not a hidden meaning that a word contains, or an already formed but unuttered thought. Merleau-Ponty explains that speech "presents or rather it is the subject's taking up of a position in the world of his meanings."[34] As we will see below, if language expresses the subject, there are times in which a failure to speak or an inability to speak *also* expresses the subject.

Merleau-Ponty's examination of Schneider's dysfunctions in his speech and sexuality is relevant here because he is rethinking Schneider's combat injuries. First, in so doing, he provides a vivid illustration of the way that human beings are embodied beings-in-the-world (over and against the Cartesian dualist model). Second, and by extension, his analysis and re-thinking of Schneider's combat injuries reveals something about the nature of injury itself. Namely, injuries happen to *embodied beings*, not just parts of bodies.

It follows, then, that a robust understanding of injury must take the human being as a whole *and* her specific experience of her situation into account. What we see in the phenomenological analysis of speech and sexuality is that "all human 'functions,' from sexuality to motility and intelligence, are rigorously unified in one synthesis."[35] If all human functions are united in one synthesis, and if Schneider's injuries can *only* be fully understood when examined from a phenomenological and holistic viewpoint, it follows that the phenomenological viewpoint could enhance understanding of *any* human injury. As we saw in the previous chapter, while it is true that the sciences provide very important information about an injury or disorder, it is a grave mistake to assume that they present the whole story.

Merleau-Ponty holds that the mistake lies in attempting to view injury by means of dissection. Impotence is construed as a malfunction in the brain *or* the body. Aphasia is understood to be *simply* a result of misfiring synapses. Traumatic memory is thought to be *just* a problem in the amygdala and hippocampus. While by no means *false*, these biological explanations clearly fall short of giving us a full account of what is going on. Schneider and his symptoms are paradigmatic of Merleau-Ponty's contention that looking at human beings with the scientific gaze from above treats the patient like an object. This gaze from above neglects to take into account the dynamism of existence—the importance of the situation and the particular subject within it—and accordingly fails to fully understand the phenomena.

What the phenomenological perspective adds to the defining and treatment of trauma is an appreciation of the need to understand what the original traumatic event(s) and the subsequent chronic symptoms *mean* to the person suffering from them. In both the case of Schneider's sexual inertia and his aphasia, the phenomenological approach furthers the understanding of the injuries by emphasizing the ways in which they involve his being-in-the-world. Rather than focusing on symptoms and the etiology behind them, phenomenology attempts to investigate the contexts within which the symptoms appear. Injury cannot be understood as *just* a particular malfunction of a part of the body or the brain. What we see so vividly in Merleau-Ponty's analysis of Schneider is that injury happens to the *entire* being. If, in keeping with this insight, we want to come to a robust understanding of a particular injury, we must take the context in which it occurs into account.

Phenomenology does more than provide a platform for understanding the nature of injury as a meaningful and personally embodied experience. When we stop being reductionist, the field of injury and trauma opens up and things are revealed that were previously obscured. One of those things is the impulse to adaptation. If we understand that when injured, the embodied being has an impulse to adapt to that injury, we will better understand the roots of trauma.

THE REFLECTED ROOM: THE PHENOMENOLOGY OF ADAPTATION

In the most general sense, the capacity to adapt refers to an organism's ability to cope with or adjust to fluctuations within her body and/or in her environment. Adaptation is a condition for the possibility of survival. If we were not able to adjust our body temperature in accordance with the temperature in the environment, for example, we would not survive.

Here, I'll talk about adaptation in two different ways. The first is what Merleau-Ponty calls the "vital impulse" toward adaptation. By this, he means something like the innate impulse to keep ourselves alive and as balanced as we can. The second kind of adaptation is adaptation gone awry, or more simply, maladaptation. This might happen when someone survives a traumatic event—there is the impulse to adapt to the situation and stay alive—and then that impulse does not get shut off and manifests as the symptoms of PTSD. What is critical to keep in mind is that maladaptation, though it can become problematic, is still rooted within the very same impulse as successful adaptation.

Adding these two things to our understanding of traumatic injury deepens our understanding of it in two crucial ways. First, we can understand that the impulse to adapt is folded in to the experience of traumatic injury. Second, we can see that though this impulse to adapt can lead to maladaptation or symptoms, this impulse is borne of strength and is not rooted in weakness.

ADAPTATION AS A VITAL IMPULSE

I want to begin the discussion of the vital impulse to adapt in what may seem like a strange place, the field of optics. In the late 1800s and early 1900s, psychologist George Stratton conducted a series of experiments on vision. At the time, prevalent theories of vision held that the retinal image was inverted in order to perceive things as upright.[36] In an attempt to test whether inversion of an image was necessary for proper vision, Stratton developed a lens that substituted "an upright retinal image for the normal inverted one."[37] Stratton first wore the lens himself and recorded his findings. In the beginning of his experiment, he noted that normal perception and movement was basically impossible, as everything in Stratton's visual field (including the movements of his own limbs) appeared to be upside down.[38] He writes his first-personal experience.

> All images at first appeared to be inverted; the room and all in it seemed upside down. The hands when stretched out from below into the visual field seemed to enter from above. Yet although these images were clear and definite, they did not at first seem to be real things, like the things we see in normal vision, but they seemed to be misplaced, false, or illusory images between the observer and the objects or the things themselves.[39]

When Stratton tried to move around in this surreal upside-down world, he found that he could only complete movements effectively when he did not rely on his vision at all, but instead relied on memory and touch, as one might when they move around in the dark. Stratton wore the lens for three days and found that he gradually learned how to navigate in the upside-down world, and accordingly, the surreal feeling of things being misplaced, false, or illusory began to fade.

On the second day, Stratton reports that he began to realize that part of the difficulty he was encountering seemed to arise from the fact that visual and tactual contacts were not being reported "perceptionally together."[40] In other words, the reason that things appeared surreal and upside down when he first put on the lens was because the visual world did not match the tactile one. He was receiving two contradictory sets of data. As a result of this experience, Stratton surmised that there were two distinct inputs for sense data—visual and tactile. The eventual adaptation of the subject to this reversed world, he argued, could only be explained through the idea that at some point during the experiment, the visual and tactile world merged resulting in the cessation of the false and surreal experience of the world.[41]

Merleau-Ponty rejects Stratton's explanation of the phenomena, calling it "unintelligible."[42] It is unintelligible, he explains, because it demands a view of the world in which a person is perceiving (or misperceiving) "real space," or one in which "the 'upright' and the 'inverted' are relationships dependent upon the fixed points chosen."[43] In other words, the problem with Stratton's conclusion is that it focuses on the objective perspective of the external world rather than the perspective of the person living through the experience.

Merleau-Ponty argues that the reason that a person eventually comes to be able to navigate the reversed world is *not* because her visual and tactile perspectives *integrate*, but because in time, she becomes capable of adapting to her situation as a being-in-the-world.

Citing a similar experiment done with mirrors, Merleau-Ponty explains the way that a subject adapts to the surroundings in the following way.

> After a few minutes . . . *the reflected room miraculously calls up a subject capable of living in it.* This virtual body ousts the real one to such an extent that the subject no longer has the feeling of being in the world where he actually is, and that instead of his real legs and arms, he feels that he has the legs and arms he would need to walk and act in the reflected room: *he inhabits the spectacle.*[44]

What the scientific explanation offered by Stratton fails to do is take the subject *as she exists within her world* into account (thus, not a disembodied, Cartesian subject, but a person living through the experience). It is not that this experience happens to a body or to a brain. The experience, like any human experience, happens to a unified, embodied, being-in-the-world. The subject does not learn to integrate her senses. Rather, she eventually adapts in order to continue to engage with the world. This happens almost miraculously—the reflected room seems to suddenly call up a subject capable of living in it. Movement, then, is not reducible to mechanics because it is about possibility and meaning.

Merleau-Ponty cites Stratton's own research for proof of this. It is important to note, he says, that within Stratton's own description, the more active the subject is, the more quickly he adapts to his surreal surroundings. This suggests to Merleau-Ponty that it is not a matter of letting two opposing representations integrate, but that "it is the experience of movement guided by sight which teaches the subject to harmonize the visual and tactile data."[45] In other words, Merleau-Ponty agrees that more effective movement becomes possible when visual and tactile data harmonize. However, he suspects that this harmony emerges as a result of a person existing in and engaging with her world. The more she interacts with the world, the more possible the world becomes for her.

This may seem like a small distinction, but it is *critical.* Where Stratton holds that the world becomes navigable when two distinct faculties unite independent of the subject's strivings, Merleau-Ponty holds that *the experience of the subject—personal, lived experience—is always a unity*. The drastic change in perception experienced by the subject who wears the glasses does not *divide* the visual from the tactile but changes her experience of being-in-the-world. Harmony becomes possible again when the subject—as a unity—adapts to her surroundings and the reflected room emerges anew.

What do these experiments about vision have to do with trauma? What they reveal is that the embodied being-in-the-world has a tremendous capacity for and impulse toward adaptation. Regardless of the accuracy of his conclusions, what is stunning about Stratton's experiments is that when someone's horizon or perceptual field is literally flipped upside down, she can completely adapt *within just a few days*. This reveals what Merleau-Ponty elsewhere calls the "impulse of being-in-the-world."[46] The impulse of being-in-the-world can be understood as the inclination to adapt when one's typical modes of existence are thwarted or altered. This impulse is vital—primal, foundational—it is what drives a person to move toward harmony when her situation becomes dissonant, and it provides crucial insight to the nature of injury.

In order to explain this vital impulse within the embodied being to adapt, Merleau-Ponty discusses injury and adaptation on the miniscule scale of a simple insect. One of the most essential ways in which an insect engages with the world (if not *the* essential way) is through movement. If the ability to move is hindered in some way, the insect will attempt to make some adjustments so that it can continue to move. In fact, the *way* that the insect adjusts will depend on *how* its movement has been altered. For example, if the insect has one of its legs tied back away from use, Merleau-Ponty points out that it does not attempt to substitute a sound leg for the missing one. He argues that this is because the leg that cannot be used is not *exactly* missing. Instead, it "continues to count in the insect's scheme of things . . . because the current of activity which flows towards the world still passes through it."[47] In this case, the body schema has been slightly altered but not changed. The insect then adapts by "simply continuing to belong in the same world and move in it with all its powers."[48]

In other words, the way that the insect adapts to these bodily challenges illustrates the way that the insect experiences the world as an embodied being. Though we would certainly not say that the insect is conscious in the same way that human beings are, the fact that it is somehow aware that the missing leg is not gone shows the prevalence of embodiment in the natural world. Even something as simple as an insect is embodied; and further; a crucial part of its embodied existence has to do with its specific situation and with the way that it engages with the world around it. If the same insect has one of its legs completely amputated, on the other hand, it *does* substitute a sound leg for the missing one. In this case, then, it seems that the insect has some bodily awareness that the missing leg is really gone this time; that it no longer counts in its body schema, and so the method of adaptation is accordingly different.

In either case, the adaptive mechanism reveals an inclination to continue being-in-the-world, to continue belonging to and engaging with the world in a similar way. Prior to the injury, the insect navigated through the world with the use of a certain number of legs in a certain order. Now missing one of those legs, the insect faces a problem; the context in which it once existed is the same, but the insect can no longer operate within it in the same way. Just as Stratton experienced with his inversion lens, the world suddenly becomes nearly impossible to navigate. However, when an embodied being has its embodiment challenged, there is an *instinctual impulse to adapt.* As Merleau-Ponty explains of the insect, "What is found behind the phenomenon of substitution is the impulse of being-in-the-world."[49] The instinctual action of attempting to correct for the injury in order to continue existing within one's world represents a kind of urge, drive, or compulsion to adapt that is inherent within embodiment.

It is tempting to say that adaptation is not unique to embodied beings. After all, inanimate objects adapt to force, but we would not say that they are conscious or embodied. They do not belong to a world or find themselves in a situation in the same way that animate beings do. To illustrate the difference between animate and inanimate objects, think about the difference between the insect and a drop of oil. We can imagine placing a drop of oil on a table and then tilting the tabletop. The oil will predictably roll to the lowest edge, and thus seems to be adapting in a similar way that the insect is. There is an important difference, however.

> The difference is simply that the drop of oil adapts itself to given external forces, while the insect *itself projects the norms of its environment and itself lays down the terms of its vital problem.*[50]

There is no projection in the oil, no conscious intentionality. The oil does not belong to an environment, and it does not have a vital problem. Indeed, only vital beings can have vital problems. To be sure, an insect is much simpler than a human being, and Merleau-Ponty is quick to point this out. That being said, there is an important way in which an insect is a being-in-the-world and not just an object. A drop of oil could be said to adapt to external forces because it moves when the table is tilted, but this is purely passive and involves no input on behalf of the oil. The oil moves or adapts itself *only* when it is acted upon. Further, the drop of oil never *has* a world in the same way that an insect does, and therefore cannot decide between two modes of adaptation. The insect belongs to a world, finds itself in a situation, and actively responds to that situation based on the experience and needs of its body.

The insect finds itself "in an 'open' situation" which "requires the animal's movements."[51] When the insect reacts to an injury by either substituting a missing leg or simply trying to continue to move about when a leg is tied back, there is a dynamic interaction with the world that cannot be present for an inanimate object like the drop of oil. Put another way, the drop of oil *is acted on by* external forces in the world; the insect *acts within* the world. The movement of the former is of necessity, while the movement of the latter is contingent. What is similar, then, for the human being and the insect, is that they are both embodied beings that belong to their worlds, and that when their being-in-the-world is interrupted through injury they will experience an impulse to adapt.

Just because there is this impulse to adapt, this does not guarantee that the mode of adaptation will always be a successful one. Human adaptation to injury is admittedly much more complicated than insect adaptation to injury. Like the insect, though, a human being can adapt in various ways to injuries, some of which are productive and some of which are not. Proof of the impulse to adapt can "show up" in many different ways—some of them show up as symptoms of the initial trauma, which provided the necessity to adapt in the first place. There are two examples of this in Merleau-Ponty's work that I will examine here. The first is the example of phantom limb syndrome. The second is an example of mutism in a case of psychological trauma.

ADAPTATION AND THE PHANTOM LIMB

Merleau-Ponty uses the simple example of the insect to provide a way to begin to understand a particularly complicated human adaptive phenomenon, phantom limb syndrome. This syndrome, common and well documented, occurs when an individual still feels sensation (most often pain or discomfort) in a limb that has been amputated.

As Merleau-Ponty points out, phantom limb syndrome cannot be explained by the psychology or physiology of his day. Thus, he finds himself compelled "to form the idea of an organic thought through which the relation of the 'psychic' to the 'physiological' becomes conceivable."[52] In other words, a syndrome like this can *only* be understood through the lens of phenomenology.

Phantom limb syndrome is an excellent illustration of the curious ways in which embodied beings sometimes attempt to adapt to injury. Not identifiable simply as a mistake in the brain, phantom limb syndrome represents an attempt on behalf of the amputee to continue interacting with the world in the way that she did prior to the injury. The sensations within the missing limb then can be understood as representing a refusal or inability to accept the radically different body schema presented after the injury. This viewpoint enables a much different understanding of the phenomena. As Merleau-Ponty explains:

> What it is in us which refuses mutilation and disablement is an I committed to a certain physical and inter-human world, who continues to tend towards his

> world despite handicaps and amputations, and who, to this extent, does not recognize them *de jure*.[53]

In other words, we might explain the presence of the phantom limb as an attempt to adapt through refusal: the individual has sustained an injury that has so drastically altered her body schema that she has become unrecognizable to herself. The "I" is committed to a world in which her limbs are intact, so the "I" then refuses to acknowledge the loss, continuing the count the limb as if it were intact. Presumably, phantom limb syndrome is so common because human beings are, as Merleau-Ponty points out, so committed to a certain bodied physical reality.

If we want to understand the way in which an individual adapts to an injury, consciously or unconsciously, bodily or psychologically, we must locate their adaptation within the context of the individual and what the injury means to them. What the injury and adaptive method *mean* are crucial pieces of the puzzle. As Merleau-Ponty explains,

> To have a phantom arm is to remain open to all the actions of which the arm alone is capable; it is to retain the practical field which one enjoyed before mutilation. The body is the vehicle of being in the world, and having a body is, for a living creature, to be intervolved in a definite environment, to identify oneself with certain projects and be continually committed to them.[54]

It is not, then, that the individual is consciously refusing to accept that the limb is gone or that there is some purely neurobiological reason that phantom limb occurs. Rather, the individual continues to see herself as having a body—and existing within a certain environment and involved in certain projects in that environment—with all four limbs. Injuries do not happen just to limbs, they happen to people, and people who take themselves to be partially constituted by their bodies. In order to understand injury and adaptation to injury, the *meaning* of the injury and adaptive method to the individual must be taken into account.[55]

To be in the world is to be more or less fragilely—indeed, mortally—anchored to a certain environment, to belong thus to a world, to find oneself within a particular situation. This anchoring entails that adaptation is a vital part of existence. If human beings did not adapt to their ever-changing surroundings, survival would be impossible. It also follows that adaptive methods will differ, depending upon the person and her specific environment.

The phenomenological lens allows us to focus on (a) the embodied character of the response to injury, (b) the adaptive character of that response (whether ultimately productive or unproductive), and (c) the particular situation, that is, the context, of both the injury and method of adapting to it.

However, as we see in the case of PTSD and phantom limb syndrome, it is not enough to just note *that* human beings adapt, it is also necessary to examine *how*. In doing so, important insights into the adaptive mechanisms that surround injury can be discovered. As discussed in chapter 2, the traumatic response that leads to PTSD is itself an adaptive process. On a neurological level, the organism reorganizes functioning in order to better respond to terror as a result of being aware of an overwhelming situation. In some cases, this reorganization promotes effective response and survival in the moment and the organism is able to return to normal functioning. In other cases, however, this series of adaptive responses becomes chronic and stands in the way of successful integration. In this case, adaptation becomes maladaptive—but it is crucial to remember that the root of what may become maladaptive is a vital impulse to adapt, to survive. The traumatic response then is fundamentally rooted in *strength*, not weakness.

Understanding the role of adaptation to trauma is so crucial because it allows the mechanism behind PTSD to be reframed as an adaptive, empowering one, rather than one that is indicative of cognitive failure or psychological weakness. Understanding PTSD as rooted in the impulse to adapt can also help radically reframe the way that we approach healing. To begin with, if PTSD is a result of adaptation to a terrifying situation in the world, it does not make sense to attempt to *cure* someone of it. One cannot be cured of their situation. Instead, treatment can become focused on using the adaptive impulse that is already there to adjust to the new situation in a more productive way.

ADAPTING TO TRAUMA

As another example of the impulse to adapt gone awry, I want to turn to an example of a patient treated by Ludwig Binswanger which Merleau-Ponty reframes in his own work. The case study involves a young woman who had been diagnosed with hysteria and admitted to Bellevue asylum in Switzerland in 1935. Her symptoms involved her mouth and throat; she could not speak or eat and would often suffer from violent hiccupping attacks. In her patient history, Binswanger noted that she suffered from similar symptoms two other times in her life, once after a terrifying earthquake. The current episode seemed to have been set off when her mother forbade her from seeing her lover. The young woman had met a marine officer and wanted to marry him, but her mother thought him unfit for her.

Merleau-Ponty explains that a Freudian analysis would "connect the symptoms to the oral phase of sexual development."[56] Under this account, her muteness would be connected directly with her sexuality. The implication is that the symptom of muteness arises when her sexual desires are thwarted and cannot find outlet. Merleau-Ponty points out that to explain her symptoms this way is to reduce the girl and her symptoms to her existence as a sexual being. As we saw with his analysis of Schneider, sexuality is not a distinct biological function that can be stripped away from other human behavior. One does not have a sexual being and an expressive being and a physical being. Rather, each of these is one part of a rigorous unity. The girl's loss of her voice, then, does not just reveal something simply about her sexuality, but about her existence in the world in general. As Merleau-Ponty explains,

> What is "fixated" on the mouth is not merely sexual existence, but, *more generally, those relations with others having the spoken word as their vehicle*. In so far as the emotion elects to find its expression in loss of speech, this is because of all bodily functions speech is the most intimately linked with communal existence, or, as we shall put it, with co-existence.[57]

The symptom of muteness has to do with "those relations with others having spoken word as their vehicle." In other words, though both Merleau-Ponty and Freud trace the symptom to the same origin, the meaning of the symptom differs. What this hints at is that though the symptom can be traced to a singular event, the traumatic injury is much more global. Her muteness, though tied to her being cut off from her lover, is not reducible to this—what she has lost is her ability to navigate the world through speech. So, to reduce her symptoms to her sexual being and *not* take into account what else the symptoms might mean is to miss a key part of the phenomena. What her symptoms *also* accomplish is a breaking away, a cutting off from a world which feels unfamiliar and uninhabitable.

In other words, rather than simply expressing an unexpressed sexual desire or drive, the young woman's symptoms also express her inability to communicate with the world in the way that she desires, and to coexist with her family and her lover. She loses her voice *not* because she suddenly loses access to words, or even that words cannot adequately express what she is experiencing, but because the impediment that is placed upon her interrupts her way of being-in-the-world. She had imagined a world not only in which she could be with her partner, but one in which her family could coexist and her mother has shattered that possibility. She cannot accept this current world and therefore cannot communicate in it. She adapts through silence. Merleau-Ponty speculates further that the reason she experienced these same symptoms after the earthquake is because she felt a similar break with coexistence, sparked by the sudden and unavoidable presence of her own mortality.[58]

What Merleau-Ponty adds to Binswanger's analysis of this young woman is the understanding that she was suffering from a rupture within her methods of communication with others in her world, and that this is the root of her mutism. It is his phenomenological perspective, which sees the patient as a whole being within a particular context, that allows him to expand on Binswanger's analysis. Similarly, when Stratton put on his retinal image reversal lens, the world turned upside down. He adapted to it by continuing to move about in the world however he could until it felt right side up again. As discussed above, his experience reveals the tremendous power within human beings to adapt. Noting the general impulse and capacity for adaptation does not, however, enable us to predict how adaptation will occur. It is just as possible to imagine an individual adapting to the reversal of their retinal image by freezing entirely, becoming completely incapable of engaging with a world that feels impossible to navigate. It is also possible to imagine someone closing their eyes and adapting by learning how to use the other senses to navigate the world that is no longer visually available. In each of these cases, the impulse of being-in-the-world, or the impulse to adapt is manifested in a different way depending on the particular person and her particular situation.

The phenomenological perspective can reframe the discussion of PTSD then, by focusing on what the symptoms mean to the particular subject experiencing them, rather than how they fit within a general diagnostic framework. In this case, it is not enough to know *that* the girl is experiencing these symptoms, and *that* they can be classified as hysterical. Merleau-Ponty's analysis begins with her existence as an embodied being-in-the-world, and the result is an understanding of the symptoms that extends much further into the experience, hinting at different origins and the more global extent of the traumatic injury. When this new perspective is added to those that already exist, the result is a more robust and multidimensional understanding of the phenomenon.

Further, this case reveals the way in which a being-in-the-world has an impulse to adapt when its typical methods of engaging with the world are altered or thwarted. In this case, the girl adapts to her injury by losing her voice. Incidentally, in keeping with Merleau-Ponty's interpretation when the impediment is removed, and the young woman is again allowed to see her lover, she becomes able to speak and all other symptoms fade away. The world becomes possible for her again, and so she regains her ability to communicate with it.

It is important to note that under Merleau-Ponty's analysis it is not the case that the young woman *chooses* these symptoms, or *willingly* loses her voice. Rather, the symptoms are enacted by and in her body.

> The sick girl does not mime with her body a drama played out "in her consciousness." By losing her voice she does not present a public version of an "inner state." . . . To have lost one's voice is not to keep silence: one keeps silence only when one can speak. It is true that loss of voice is not paralysis. . . . Yet neither

> is aphonia a deliberate or voluntary silence. . . . The girl does not cease to speak, she "loses" her voice as one loses a memory.[59]

The symptoms are not choices she makes in order to manipulate the world back into what it once was. Rather, they represent her existence within her particular situation.[60] It is the perception that hysterical or traumatic symptoms are a choice that has led to the mistreatment of so many traumatized patients. Recall the cases treated by Yealland mentioned in chapter 1. Yealland believed that the symptoms did not authentically express the patients' experience. He believed instead that the symptoms represented weakness, a lack of morale. This belief led him to treat his patients abusively, and when they were "cured" of their muteness, he credited his own hypothesis for the success.

Merleau-Ponty might have surmised that the soldiers were mute because they could no longer communicate within a world that contained such atrocities as the ones they encountered and participated in at war. Or that they could not speak what they had experienced, which was so shattering that it challenged their previous beliefs about the world. He might conclude that the halting and staccato movements of their bodies were a result of their inability to continue freely moving in a world that was so physically violent. He also might conclude that Yealland's methods were successful because they presented a situation that was so terrifying for the soldiers that they abandoned their symptoms out of necessity, not because they had been cured, snapped out of it, or and reminded of their moral and heroic natures.

CONCLUSION

In the previous chapter, I argued that the phenomenological perspective adds a critical layer to what has been established in neuroscience and psychology when it comes to understanding trauma and traumatic memory. By taking into account the lived experience of the victim, and understanding traumatic memory as not just a problem in the brain, but a result of one's horizon being altered due to traumatic experience, Merleau-Ponty's phenomenological perspective allows us to reframe the discussion of traumatic memory in important ways.

This chapter has expanded this discussion into one of traumatic injury in general by further examining the way that traumatic experience can alter one's being-in-the-world. Beginning with Merleau-Ponty's analysis of Schneider, it was argued that the phenomenological perspective can give insight into just what has been injured by taking into account the embodied person as a whole and the context in which the symptoms appear. In regards to the trauma response, taking into account both the generalizable symptoms exhibited as well as the specific context in which they arise and take form has crucial implications for understanding and treatment. It explains why two soldiers who experienced the same event during combat might both have PTSD but exhibit completely different symptoms. This is because it locates the injury in the adaptive impulse of the individual, which is shaped by that particular individual's unique way of being-in-the-world. Finally, it hints that what is injured in trauma is not simply one's memory, but the way one exists in and apprehends the world entirely.

This is not simply a different way to think about PTSD, rather, it reveals that there is a root system of meaning in traumatic experience. The way that trauma can shatter one's structure of meaning is not something that we currently focus on in treatment. We see that in reducing symptoms to singular explanations becomes a barrier to understanding and treating PTSD. When we only have a part of the story, we can only address a part of the problem.

NOTES

1. Kardiner, *Traumatic Neuroses of War*, 74.
2. Ibid., 74.
3. For a thorough summary and critical analysis of Schneider's case, see Georg Goldenberg, "Goldstein and Gelb's Case Schn: A Classic Case in Neuropsychology?" in *Brain, Behavior and Cognition: Classic Cases in Neuropsychology, Volume II*, eds. Chris Code, Claus-W. Wallesch, Yves Joanette, and Andre Roch Lecours (Florence: Psychology Press, 2013), 281–299. Beyond giving background of Schneider's case, Goldenberg argues that the doctors that treated Schneider, Kurt Goldstein and Adhemar Gelb, manipulated the patient into expressing some of the symptoms that they cited, rendering the case invalid. Other theorists have suggested that rather than dismiss the research, that the case be re-examined in light of current research. See, for example, J. J. Marotta and M. Behrman, "Patient Schn: Has Goldstein and Gelb's Case Withstood the Test of Time?" *Neuropsychologia* 42 (2004): 633–638. Regardless of any controversy that surrounds Schneider's case, what is relevant here is Merleau-Ponty's analysis of his symptoms and not the validity of the symptoms themselves. Especially, given the fact that the symptoms that Schneider displays are common among veterans with his injuries.
4. Max C. Dillon, *Merleau-Ponty's Ontology* (Bloomington: Indiana University Press, 1988), 131.
5. Merleau-Ponty, *Phenomenology of Perception*, 90.
6. Ibid., 78.
7. Ibid., xii.
8. Dillon, *Merleau-Ponty's Ontology*, 132.
9. Maurice Merleau-Ponty, *The Structure of Behavior*, trans. Alden L. Fisher (Pittsburgh: Duquesne, 1983), 148.

10. Ibid., 147. There is a rich discussion in the literature about embodiment and agency. At the center of this is the question of the extent to which individuals have ownership over their actions. The debate about the status of non-intentional movements and thoughts in particular has been recently taken up in the fields of phenomenology, cognitive science, and neuroscience. See, for example, Shaun Gallagher, "On the Possibility of Naturalizing Phenomenology," in *The Oxford Handbook of Contemporary Philosophy*, ed. Dan Zahavi (New York: Oxford University Press, 2012), 70–93, and see especially 82–87.

11. It is crucial to note that Merleau-Ponty is grappling with the state of science as it was in the mid-nineteenth century. It is important to keep in mind the limitations of technology at this time, as well as the technological advancements that have been made since.

12. Merleau-Ponty, *Phenomenology of Perception*, 179.

13. Ibid., 179–180.

14. Ibid., emphasis added.

15. It is worth mentioning that the Merleau-Ponty does not explain the specific scientific method for determining that Schneider is biologically sexually capable. However, the specifics of Schneider's case are not as important as what Schneider is paradigmatic of, namely, that sexuality cannot be reduced to simple biological or psychological explanation.

16. It is difficult to grasp just what Merleau-Ponty means by "meaning" in his work. Provisionally, it seems like there are two main aspects to the concept. First, and simply, it seems that meaning has to do with what a particular event or situation signifies for an individual. In this sense, meaning must be intimately related to experience and embodiment for Merleau-Ponty. Recall the simple example of the child who is initially attracted to the flame of a candle, and then after getting burned by the flame comes to see it as something to avoid. It seems here that the meaning of the flame shifts with the child's experience. What it signifies has changed based on his being burned. Second, "meaning" seems to relate more abstractly to a sense of unity, or the way things pull together in perception and experience. In the discussion following a lecture that Merleau-Ponty gave in 1947, Jean Hyppolite remarked that Merleau-Ponty's work contained, "an ontology of meaning . . . which constitutes the unity of man." Maurice Merleau-Ponty, "The Primacy of Perception and Its Philosophical Consequences," trans. James M. Edie, in *The Primacy of Perception: And Other Essays on Phenomenological Psychology, the Philosophy of Art, History, and Politics*, ed. James M. Edie, authored by Maurice Merleau-Ponty (Evanston, IL: Northwestern University Press, 1964), 39. It should be noted that this remark was couched in a criticism of Merleau-Ponty's work and the discussion strayed from the topic of meaning but it seems correct to say that meaning for Merleau-Ponty is tied in with the concept of unity. It seems that meaning has to be tied to unity (in order for something to have a meaning it has to be represented in a unified way), and that this coincides with Merleau-Ponty's explanation of perception.

17. Ibid., 181.

18. Ibid.

19. Ibid.

20. Ibid., 178.
21. Ibid., 182.
22. Merleau-Ponty, *Phenomenology of Perception*, 185.
23. This is *not* to say that a full, three-dimensional understanding of an embodied injury is always necessary in the moment. It is tempting to say that there are injuries that happen to the body that are primarily and perhaps even strictly physical. A ruptured appendix might be one such example. In this case, it is not necessary for the emergency room doctor to assess the entire embodied situation of the patient in order to effectively treat her. However, it does *not* then follow that injuries happen to *bodies* in general and not *subjects*. Even the patient who suffers from the rupturing of a nonessential internal organ that previously had no impact on her bodied existence still experiences this within the context of a particular situation. Further, that rupturing doesn't just happen to her *appendix*, it happens to *her*, and therefore could be meaningful to her as a being-in-the-world in many different ways.
24. Merleau-Ponty, *Phenomenology of Perception*, 207.
25. Ibid., 209.
26. Hubert Dreyfus, "Current Relevance of Merleau-Ponty's Phenomenology of Embodiment," *Electronic Journal of Analytic Philosophy* 4 (Spring 1996): http://ejap.louisiana.edu/EJAP/1996.spring/dreyfus.1996.spring.html.
27. Merleau-Ponty, *Phenomenology of Perception*, 203, my emphasis.
28. Ibid., 225.
29. A phoneme is the smallest segment in a sound system of a language that can be contrasted with other segments. The sound /d/ that appears in both words wound and pound is an example of a phoneme.
30. For a summary of these experiments, see D. W. Carroll, *Psychology of Language, 4th Edition* (Belmont, MA: Wadsworth/Thompson, 2004), 82–87. For a detail of the experiments see A. G. Samuel, "Phonemic Restoration: Insights from a New Methodology," *Journal of Experimental Psychology* 110 (1981): 474–494. See also R. M. Warren, "Perceptual Restoration of Missing Speech Sounds," *Journal of Science* 167, no. 3917 (1970): 392–393. R. M. Warren, "Auditory Illusions and Confusions," *Scientific American* 223 (December 1970): 30–36.
31. Carroll, *Psychology of Language*, 84–85.
32. See also J. L. Elman and James L. McClelland, "Cognitive Penetration of the Mechanisms of Perception: Compensation for Co-articulation of Lexically Restored Phonemes," *Journal of Memory & Language* 27 (1988): 143–165.
33. Merleau-Ponty, *Phenomenology of Perception*, 206.
34. Ibid., 225.
35. Ibid., 222.
36. George M. Stratton, "Some Preliminary Experiments on Vision without Inversion of the Retinal Image," *Psychological Review* 3, no. 6 (November 1896): 611–617.
37. Ibid. Since the eye projects an inverted image onto the retina, Stratton's lens projects an inverted image to the eye, which projects a re-inverted image to the retina. In other words, the projection on the retina matches the objects as they are in the world (which is upside down to the brain).

38. Ibid., 613–614.
39. Ibid., 611.
40. Ibid., 615.
41. Due to the subjective nature and brevity of his preliminary experiment, Stratton performed follow-up studies that included both a longer version of this same experiment and a few variations that included mirrors instead of lenses to flesh out his hypothesis about the relationship between visual and tactile perception. See, George M. Stratton, "Vision Without Inversion of the Retinal Image," *Psychological Review* 4, no. 5 (September 1897): 463–481. See also George M. Stratton, "The Spatial Harmony of Touch and Sight," *Mind* 8, no. 32 (October 1899): 492–505.
42. Merleau-Ponty, *Phenomenology of Perception*, 287.
43. Ibid., 288.
44. Ibid., 291, emphasis added.
45. Ibid., 286.
46. Ibid., 90.
47. Ibid.
48. Ibid.
49. Ibid.
50. Ibid.
51. Ibid.
52. Ibid., 89.
53. Ibid., 94.
54. Ibid.
55. Phantom limb syndrome still perplexes researchers today. It is generally considered a maladaptive response to the physical trauma of sudden loss of a limb. See, for example, H. Knotkova, et al., "Current and Future Options for the Management of Phantom-limb Pain," *Journal of Pain Research* 5 (March 2012): 39–49; H. Flor, et al., "Phantom-limb Pain as a Perceptual Correlate of Cortical Reorganization Following Arm Amputation," *Nature* 375, no. 6531 (June 1995): 482–482; H. Flor, et al., "Phantom Limb Pain: A Case of Maladaptive Central Nervous System Plasticity?" *National Review of Neuroscience* 7, no. 11 (November 2006): 873–881.
56. Merleau-Ponty, *Phenomenology of Perception*, 186.
57. Ibid., emphasis added.
58. Ibid.
59. Ibid.
60. Ibid., 187.

Chapter 4

Trauma and the Troubled Mind

Narrative Healing, Narrative Harming

If psychology and neurobiology give us insights into what trauma is as well as how and why it manifests in disruptive symptoms, and phenomenology adds depth to their accounts, an important question remains: What can be done about it?

There is a thread that has underpinned trauma treatment since Freud and Breuer wrote *Studies on Hysteria*; this idea that in order to heal from trauma, the traumatic event must be narrated by the victim. As discussed in the prologue, when they discovered that hysterical symptoms seemed to disappear when the traumatic experience was "talked through" with the clinician, Freud and Breuer concluded that in order to heal, one must tell. Speak what feels unspeakable, and the event loses its power.

This kernel remains a mainstay in trauma therapy today, and it is at the root of the current "gold standard" therapies for combat trauma recommended by the United States Veteran's Administration. If we have a gold standard therapy for combat trauma that is based on a hypothesis that has been maintained for close to 150 years, why does combat trauma seem to resist treatment? Why are the statistics surrounding veteran suicide still so staggering? In this chapter, I examine narrative therapy from its origins with the goal of revealing the nuances of speaking what feels unspeakable, and of highlighting the dangers of forcing that speech.[1]

I do this by splitting the chapter into two parts. In the first, I consider the nuances of narrative therapy by focusing on the nature of the narrative self and considering how traumatic experience challenges (perhaps even shatters) that self. I then examine the importance of perspective taking in narrative, and how the act of occupying different perspectives on the same event can help the victim of trauma regain agency and revise meaning. Finally, I turn to the critical role of the other in the trauma narrative. In the second section, I highlight the dangers of forcing this speech by considering Prolonged Exposure Therapy alongside a more phenomenological approach. Here I make use of three case studies in order to highlight just how different these methods can be even though they share the same theoretical foundation.

THE NUANCES OF NARRATIVE

The history of the use of narrative in clinical settings begins with the study of trauma in the late 1800s. As discussed in chapter 1, in *Studies on Hysteria*, Sigmund Freud and Josef Breuer report their discovery that patients who verbalized their traumatic pasts often found profound remission of hysterical symptoms. The origin of their symptoms could be traced back to the perplexing tension between the presence and the absence of the traumatic past. Patients often did not seem to have conscious access to the specifics of their pasts, but consistently found remnants of those past events present in somatic symptoms. Freud and Breuer employed hypnotism in order to unearth what was too overwhelming to cope with in the moment and therefore had been repressed.[2] What they discovered in their examination of hysterical patients was that when the overwhelming event or events could finally be uncovered, spoken of, and connected to the bodily symptoms that the patient was suffering from, the symptoms would disappear. As noted in the prologue, Freud and Breuer themselves acknowledge that they came by this discovery largely by accident.

> For we found, to our great surprise at first, that *each individual hysterical symptom immediately and permanently disappeared when we had succeeded in bringing clearly to light the memory of the event by which it was provoked and in arousing its accompanying affect, and when the patient had described the event in the greatest possible detail and had put the affect into words.*[3]

In other words, in their work with traumatized patients, they noticed that there seemed to be something therapeutic about simply externalizing the event by means of a narrative that gave voice to the emotions that were connected to the event.

The first instance of this discovery was the case of Anna O.[4] This patient is described by Breuer as an empathetic, sensitive and intelligent woman, who began suffering from hysterical symptoms over a ten-month span in which she was caring for her dying father. During his illness, and subsequently after his death, she suffered from dissociative psychosis, alternating states of consciousness, severe headaches, a persistent squint, and intermittent paralysis of her upper and lower extremities and neck muscles among other distressing symptoms.[5]

One symptom that Breuer found particularly fascinating was that she seemed to "transfer into the past." Specifically, she would retreat into the year before her father died whenever she smelled oranges, which she had eaten almost exclusively while first taking care of him. Her perception that it was 1880 instead of 1881 was so total that she forgot nearly every detail of 1881, including the fact that she had physically moved living quarters. As Breuer describes,

> She was carried back to the previous year with such intensity that in the new house she hallucinated her old room, so that when she wanted to go to the door she kicked up against the stove which stood in the same relation to the window as the door did in the old room.[6]

Much like the veteran who hears a loud noise and is suddenly transported back to combat, in these moments when the past was ushered forward into the present, Anna O. ceased to be able to tell the difference between the past and the present.

After spending several months with her, Breuer accidentally stumbled upon a method that helped while trying to deal with one of the more urgent symptoms that had arisen, which was a complete inability to drink water. Anna O. would feel thirsty, reach for a glass of water, and then push it away, unable to drink and with no conscious understanding of why she was suddenly hydrophobic. One evening, while under hypnosis, Anna O. started to tell a story about a visit with a friend, where she witnessed this friend letting her dog drink out of her own water glass. Anna O. had felt it necessary to be polite in the moment, but while under hypnosis revealed feeling intense anger and disgust at the time. As soon as she told this story while expressing the initial anger and disgust while under hypnosis, she asked for a glass of water, drank it, and then awoke, never to experience hydrophobia again.[7] Though this particular instance of seeing a dog drink from her friend's water glass wasn't necessarily traumatic in the way that the sickness and subsequent death of her father were, it was a time in which Anna O. felt intense affect that could not be discharged, which led to an interruption in her normal functioning. The incident signaled to Breuer that there might be a way to reach Anna O. and alleviate her symptoms.

Breuer went on to take each of her symptoms and connect them with the original disturbance through conversation with Anna O. while she was under hypnosis, and he reported that as they went through this process each symptom disappeared. As he says, "In this way her paralytic contractors and anesthesia, disorders of vision and hearing of every sort, neuralgias, coughing, tremors, etc. and finally her disturbances of speech were 'talked away.'"[8]

Freud and Breuer theorized that if the patient could be convinced to talk about the traumatic event, while feeling the overwhelming emotions that were repressed, the traumatic symptoms no longer manifested themselves somatically in the patient. Since this could not often happen through regular discussion, they coaxed the narrative out while the patient was under hypnosis. They explain:

> The injured person's reaction to the trauma only exercises a completely "cathartic" effect if it is an adequate reaction . . . but *language serves as a substitute for action*; by its help, an affect could be "abreacted" almost as effectively.[9]

Emotional catharsis can occur when the narrative "serves as a substitute for action." In other words, hysterical symptoms appeared because there was some emotion or set of emotions that became internalized rather than expressed, and the internalization of unexpressed affect led to these somatic symptoms. These patients were so difficult to treat because the remnants of their pasts were constantly reenacted even though there was no immediate consciousness of the past or awareness that the past was what was causing the symptoms. The cure was to give voice to the emotion and release it, if not in action, in language and affect.

Studies on Hysteria would have us think that this "talking cure" was a panacea for hysteria. Yet, while Anna O. may have experienced some temporary relief, Breuer did not succeed in curing her and she went on to suffer continuously for several years. As mentioned in chapter 1, Freud and Breuer would go on to disavow themselves of their research entirely and set aside the subject of hysteria. Though the miraculous healing power of the talking cure was perhaps exaggerated, and their abandonment of their patients was deeply unethical, the central core of their findings seems to bear out. The truth (or accuracy) of their findings lies in the core belief that narrating the traumatic event has therapeutic power, though perhaps not for the reasons they thought.

PICKING UP THE THREAD

As discussed in previous chapters, Abram Kardiner is one clinician who attempted to rescue these core ideas from the wreckage of Freud and Breuer's work to improve the treatment of combat veterans in the 1940s. Kardiner's experience with veterans brought a few notable theoretical differences and clinical improvements to Freud and Breuer's initial work. Among these improvements was a deeper understanding of just what was helpful about talking through the traumatic event.

Freud and Breuer had thought that the success of their treatment resulted from a combination of abreaction and catharsis, that is, reliving the traumatic event and purging the repressed emotion, respectively.[10] This might be termed the abreaction/catharsis model. Again, it is based on the theory that at the heart of hysteria was an event and corresponding set of emotions that had not been expressed. These emotions, as long as they continued to go unexpressed, would continue to produce and be enacted as hysterical symptoms. That is, of course, unless the clinician could get the patient to feel and express these emotions while rendering the event into coherent narrative form.

Kardiner held on to the theory that talking through the traumatic past could be therapeutic for victims, but dismissed the explanation that results came from abreaction and catharsis. Essentially, he thought this hypothesis was too simple. He says of the abreaction/catharsis model, "The matter is not quite so simple, as may be proven from the chronic cases where abreaction by itself has no curative value."[11] If this method was as effective as Freud and Breuer thought, it should work all the time. It, of course, didn't. This led Kardiner to pull the method apart in an attempt to refine it.

Kardiner hypothesized that the mechanism behind the "talking cure" was less about a release of pent up emotion and more about acknowledging those emotions as a logical reaction to an upsetting event, and then beginning a process of "re-education of [one's] sense of reality."[12] In other words, the success of the therapy is not due to the fact that it allows patients to express some hitherto unexpressed emotion. Instead, narrative therapy was successful because talking through the traumatic event lends structure and coherence to an overwhelming experience, thereby allowing the patient to stand back from the event and re-examine the ways in which the trauma might be coloring his current experience. It also allows the patient to process her initial reaction to the trauma.

The goal of therapy for a traumatized individual under Kardiner's analysis, then, is twofold. First, the patient should be gradually made aware of the way in which he may have developed maladaptive tendencies as a result of the traumatic event. As will be illustrated in a case study below, even though the patient may understand *that* he is experiencing symptoms, the nuances of the origin and purpose of these symptoms will often evade him. Second, "every effort should be bent to re-educating the patient to the *actual realities* in which he lives rather than to the dangerous and inhospitable world in which he fancies himself."[13] In other words, the role of the clinician is to help the patient learn to differentiate between the traumatic memory and reality. Not just to serve as an exorcist of emotion. This method focuses much more on the experience of the patient—both in the initial trauma and in the therapeutic method. Once the patient has been made aware of the connections between his symptoms and past trauma, the clinician can begin to help him understand the difference between the past and present so that the patient can eventually come to see that the trauma is not repeating itself in the present.

To give an example, Kardiner describes his treatment of a patient whose main symptoms were persistent and debilitating fainting spells and nightmares. The fainting spells were preceded by "a queer sensation in the pit of his stomach," and the nightmares always involved falling from high places.[14] Kardiner reports that the patient was resistant to therapy at first, explaining that he was working hard to try and *forget* the things that Kardiner was trying to get him to remember. The patient did not feel that he was traumatized, and so accordingly thought the therapy unnecessary.

A relevant factor in his case was a plane crash that the patient had survived but had no conscious memory of. Since he was trying to push the memory of the crash away, he did not connect his current symptoms with it. Kardiner suspected that this crash was at the root of the patient's somatic symptoms.

The first step of therapy was for Kardiner to get the patient to see the ways in which his traumatic experience might be contributing to his current symptoms. Kardiner suspected that the "queer feeling in his stomach" and his nightmares of falling from high places were instances of re-experiencing the plane crash.[15] Again, since the patient had no conscious memory of the plane crash, he did not at all see the connection between his bodied memory and the past event.

When the patient became aware that the uncomfortable symptoms arose from a fear of falling that originated from a somatic memory of his plane crash, this allowed him to begin to find some distance between the past trauma and the present moment. Kardiner explains that these symptoms arise from an attempt to adapt.

> It was not very difficult to convince him of two important things. First, that all these devices he was using were defensive maneuvers of a more or less reflex and disorganized kind. And secondly, that these defensive devices were quite irrelevant to the actual world in which he was living.[16]

There are two steps to this process. The first is getting the patient to see that the symptoms are connected to the trauma. During the plane crash, when feeling the overwhelming horror of hurtling through the air, the defense mechanism was to faint. The symptom is then brought into the present when the patient is presented with any reminder of that situation—even a somatic feeling that is not tied to any conscious thought or fear. Getting the patient to see that the symptom is related serves to demystify and legitimize what feels frightening and irrational. The next step is to separate the traumatic response from current reality by normalizing the symptom and then helping the patient determine actual versus perceived threat. This defense mechanism—which may have saved the patient in the moment of the crash—had become maladaptive, as it came to accompany experiences in the world in which there was no actual danger.

Kardiner then goes on to describe the care with which he approached this patient, consistently allowing the patient to determine the pace at which they worked. Rather than putting the patient under hypnosis and coaxing the memory out, Kardiner preferred to work with fully conscious patients, arguing that abreaction under hypnosis could be violent and destructive for both the patient and the clinician.[17]

Though he did not use this word, Kardiner's method is distinctly phenomenological. It focuses on using the first-personal lived experience of the patient's trauma (and traumatic symptoms) to guide both the content and the pace of therapy. Further, the idea of re-educating the patient emerges from an understanding that traumatic symptoms are not simply instances of unexpressed emotion that need to find their way out. Rather, Kardiner was aware that what has been injured in the case of trauma is the way in which the victim sees and operates within the world (what Merleau-Ponty might call "the patient's horizon"). So in addition to giving priority to the first-personal experience of the patient, he acknowledges that trauma is disruptive because it alters the patient's phenomenal field.

To return to Breuer's patient Anna O., when she smelled oranges, her past came forward into the present. Her present experience of the world elided with her traumatic experience a year earlier, and her phenomenal field was then overtaken by the traumatic past. When the veteran felt a pit in his stomach, he was experiencing his fall all over again. Where Breuer simply saw emotional content that needed releasing, Kardiner seems to have recognized that in order to help the patient learn to differentiate from the traumatic past and the present, he needed to meet them in that experience, explain why it might be happening, and carry them out of it (as it were).

As a result of his improvements to Freud and Breuer's work, Kardiner came to redefine trauma as an injury to adaptive processes, rather than understand it as the result of interrupted affects. According to Kardiner, trauma is an injury whereby, "adaptive processes are injured, spoiled, disorganized, or shattered." Accordingly, traumatic symptoms must be understood as "new adaptations."[18] Kardiner's method of treating combat victims assumes that in order to treat the traumatized patient, one must begin by examining what sorts of maladaptive structures of meaning have been constructed out of the trauma. Kardiner explains that a patient can achieve relief from his suffering only when his "picture of the outer world has been changed, when his courage and resources in handling this new external reality have been increased or restored, at least in part, to their erstwhile state."[19] It is not enough for Anna O. to simply, say, narrate what happened while feeling overwhelming emotions under hypnosis and then have this traumatic event connected to the present symptom by the therapist (though this may have had a short-term positive effect). What Breuer failed to do was to meet her in the imagined past and *show* her the distance between the present and the past and help her relearn the feeling of safety in the present.

Kardiner's improvements on Freud and Breuer's initial theories about the talking cure then can be seen as a turning toward a clinical method with patent parallels to phenomenology. These parallels are on display in the way that Kardiner understands trauma to be an adaptive response, in his emphasis on the first-personal experience of the patient, and in his understanding of the way that trauma alters what Merleau-Ponty would call the patient's "phenomenal field."

Kardiner set the tone for the clinical understanding of combat trauma; but rather than steadily build on his foundation, different threads have emerged that have their basis in this same past. Today, there are two threads of narrative therapy that head in somewhat opposing directions. One follows the Freudian model, and the other seems to pick up where Kardiner left off. Before examining these two in juxtaposition it is important to consider more deeply why narrative is so central to this method. What is a narrative, exactly, and why is it so necessary in healing from trauma?

THE NARRATIVE SELF

It is helpful to begin with a working definition of narrative. I take a narrative to be a linguistic representation of events or sequences that occur to conscious human agents, a representation that is expressed from a particular perspective. The occurrence to conscious human agents entails degrees of coherence, continuity, and meaning. Narratives can apply to conscious human agents collectively (as in the case of communities) or to individuals. This entailment explains why narratives help us understand, relate to, and file away the things that happen to us and to those around us. Though it is of course possible to tell completely fictional narratives, the kind of narratives that are at play here are personal narratives in so far as they are about people and the events in their lives.

There are a few essential things to note in this definition. First, a narrative is more than a simple list or chronicle but does not need to necessarily have strong and coherent causation—both coherence and causation occur in degrees. Second, it is linguistic, meaning that its form is language, rather than music or painting for example—but it can be thought through and not necessarily spoken or written. Third, it is crucial to notice the interplay between the subjective perspective and the objective world in which the events that are narrated occur. A narrative cannot ever be purely objective because it is always a representation that comes from a particular perspective. This means that on some level, all narratives are colored both by the perspectives within them and the perspective of the person telling them.

However, it is crucial to note that it does *not* follow that all narratives are then false. Since a narrative is defined here as a representation of an event or sequence of events, it has important ties to the objective world. Both the objective reality of the event and the perspective of the person who lived through it and is now telling a story about it are necessary and important. Although sometimes the objective reality of the events and the representation of the events match nearly perfectly, there is still quite a bit of space between them. As we will see in more detail below, navigating the space between representation and reality is indeed one of the tasks of narrative as an adaptive tool in the case of trauma.

Any therapeutic method that relies on narrative (e.g., psychotherapy, cognitive behavioral therapy, narrative exposure therapy, etc.) rests on the belief that personal identity is partially constituted by narratives that we tell about ourselves and that other people tell about us. Implicit in this idea is the assumption that human psychology is narratively structured such that we perceive and communicate occurrences in narrative form. If this is how human psychology is structured, it then follows that processing the events in our lives requires that we render them in narrative form. How we render them—the content, shape, and cadence of our stories—in turn can transform the way that we relate to particular events in our lives.

The extent to which an individual's personal reality is constructed narratively is something that varies within the field of psychology. Radical constructivists, for example, hold that objective reality is inaccessible, and therefore the *only* version of reality that is relevant is the one that is created by the neurological structure of the individual human brain. Social constructivists, on the other hand, hold that reality—and by extension personal identity—is a social construction, and therefore that meaning is constructed socially. Critical constructivists also hold that reality is created socially, but they also believe that the mind can intervene and assign new meaning to that reality.[20] Though approaches differ based on which of these ideologies a clinician finds herself aligning with, all narrative approaches to therapy agree that *who we are* is in some important way a result of the stories that we tell about our past and future (and perhaps the stories that other people tell about us).

Under this account, psychological angst can often be attributed to fissures in the story or stories that a patient is telling about herself and her life.[21] So it is not the case that one simply needs to tell the story in order to heal (as Freud and Breuer suspected), but that integrating the story into one's larger narrative is also necessary. In other words, it's not as simple as just saying what happened out loud. Rather, saying what happened out loud marks the beginning of the process in which the narrator can assign meaning to the event and relate it to the larger narrative about her life.

There is a tension in narrating traumatic events in that they call out to be narrated and simultaneously seem to resist narrative. As we have seen, a part of what constitutes traumatic experience is that it feels unspeakable. Though narrating the traumatic event is the locus of the problem, the solution is to use the malleability of narrative structure in order to tell the stories so that they *do* match up with and/or adequately express their experience. This empowers the patient to take control of the past by rendering into narrative form, and also to determine her own meaning of the events in the past.[22] Narrating also provides a critical distance between the event in the past and the current moment. In order for the patient to render the events of the past in narrative form, she must step into the narrator position; a position that enables her to tell the story from a new temporal perspective. The narrator position is one in which what happened must be placed in the past, rather than simply relived. The narrator occupies the present moment and speaks of the past as a distinct and distant thing. In so doing, the narrator has the opportunity to both report what happened, and also to create or revise the meaning of what happened.[23] This need not happen only once, the event can be recreated and revised as time goes on. In the same way that objects appear different as we move away from them, so, too, can the events of our lives have different meanings at different times.

It is important to understand that though we may talk about our lives using narrative structure, this does not mean that our lives are *literally* narratives, rather that they are *narratable*. Eugene Gendlin's concept of the felt-implicit is helpful here. The felt-implicit is the embodied experience that an individual has in the moment. It is pre-conceptual and remains so unless the subject finds a reason to articulate it through language—which she can choose to do at any time. Gendlin argues that meaning creation occurs when lived experience (which though it is implicit it always carries with it the possibility of being made explicit) becomes explicit and meaningful through the use of language.[24] In other words, our lived experience is immediate and inarticulate, and it becomes archived as meaningful in a particular way when we put language to our experience. This process of putting experience into language enables the subject to engage with the world as a relatively stable self because as she archives events, she determines the importance of events and the meanings that they carry for her. Gendlin goes even further to argue that the way that the story is told and what it then means for the subject can change her experience of the external world.

For example, if I were to tell you a story about a time when I nearly drowned after falling into a swimming pool at the age of five, I do so from a great distance from that event. In fact, there are two entirely distinct perspectives. There is the "I" that is situated in the present moment, this is the perspective from which I am telling the story. There is also the "me" within the story, the person who experienced the event and (in some sense) remains within it. When I tell this story, I am able to recognize myself in *that past*, and I am also able to give an account of what this story means for me in *this present*. Since *this present* is fleeting, the meaning of the story may change as I tell it in different times of my life. In this way I am able to assign and revise the meaning that events have, even though I cannot change what those events are. It is the capacity for assigning and revising meaning that enables me to integrate the past with the larger narrative of my life.

Again, under this account of narrative and selfhood, what is so problematic about traumatic events is precisely that they resist this kind of integration. One is either unable to gain the necessary perspective to separate between the past and present ("me" versus "I," respectively) or she is not able to entirely take up the perspective of the narrator "I" who is able to fully recognize that the event happened and is not still happening. In order to understand this more thoroughly, we must look more closely at what perspective taking in narration accomplishes.

THE IMPORTANCE OF PERSPECTIVE TAKING

Peter Goldie argues for the power of language in the face of trauma.[25] His position is that since human beings are situated in time, there is a natural tendency to reflect on our pasts and project ourselves into the future. One of the ways that we do this is through rendering our thoughts into narrative form. Most relevant here is the way that his characterization of a narrative focuses on the way that narratives can provide opportunities for the subject to assign meaning and explore alternative perspectives on events.

> A narrative is . . . a representation of events which is shaped, organized, and colored, presenting those events, and the people involved in them, from a certain perspective or perspectives, and thereby giving narrative structure—coherence, meaning, and evaluative and emotional import—to what is related.[26]

Successful narratives, according to Goldie, contain all three of these attributes. Coherence "reveals causal connections to the audience in a way that a mere list or chronicle would not." A narrative is meaningful insofar as it "enables the audience to understand how the actions of those persons who are internal to the narrative could have made sense to them at the time." Emotional import refers to "the narrator's external evaluation of, and emotional response to, what happened, from the ironic distance that his external perspective allows."[27]

Goldie argues that narratives are essential because they enable us to represent events from the past from a variety of different temporal perspectives.

To illustrate the way that two perspectives appear in any simple narrative, he gives the following example. "Last night, in the dark, I tripped over because a suitcase had been left in the hall whilst I was out shopping."[28] Even in this minimalist story, there are two distinct perspectives: that of Goldie internal to the story (this is the "me" perspective, he refers to it as the lower-level perspective), tripping over a suitcase that he did not realize was in the way; and that of Goldie external to the story, telling the narrative now with the benefit of hindsight (this is the "I" perspective, which he terms the higher-level perspective).

Notice that the higher-level perspective contains information that the lower-level perspective does not have access to. For example, the higher-level "I" perspective is aware of what was tripped over, while the lower-level "me" perspective is not. There is also a certain level of flexibility when it comes to meaning and emotional evaluation in the higher-level "I" perspective of the narrator that is not available to the subject inside the narrative. From the point of view of the lower-level "me" perspective, when Goldie tripped over the suitcase he likely felt startled and experienced physical pain. He might have been subsequently frustrated and annoyed. From the higher-level "I" perspective that he gains when telling the story, he might now find it humorous. He might imagine himself unknowingly stumbling around in the dark and feel foolish about his decision not to turn on the lights. He might imagine his wife leaving the suitcase in the hallway and feel anger and resentment. When he tells the story three weeks later, the anger and resentment he felt in the days following the event might have turned into amusement.[29]

Though this is a very simple narrative, it is already evident that to tell or think through any narrative, one must step into the higher-level perspective in order to tell the story. In order to tell the story about tripping over the suitcase, Goldie has to "stand back from [his] earlier self, acentrally imagining the scene unfold."[30] This act is one not of fictionalizing, but of observing. Goldie is not rewriting or falsifying the past, but rather witnessing what occurred from the vantage point of the higher-level perspective. What this viewpoint allows is the opportunity to reevaluate one's emotional response to the events.

Imagine, for example, that upon tripping over the suitcase in the hallway, Goldie flew into a rage and woke up his wife and screamed at her for several hours, admonishing her for being so careless. In the moment, this emotional response seemed appropriate to him. In telling the story, the next day to a friend, Goldie would be forced to stand back from his earlier self and, in so doing, has the opportunity to reevaluate that response. He might, perhaps, decide that his emotional response was exaggerated and out of control, prompting him to apologize to his wife.

As is evident in this example, the higher-level perspective is powerful because of its flexibility. In telling the story, and inhabiting a higher-level perspective, the subject can look critically at the meaning that the event carries for her. This cannot be done from the lower-level perspective because what is available to the subject internal to the story is only the emotion that was initially attached to the event. Narratives are crucial to our lives, then, because they allow us to embody an alternate point of view, one that enables us to engage with the past from a certain distance if not with a certain objectivity.[31] From this alternate point of view, we are in a position to determine whether or not a particular emotional response was appropriate. If there is rewriting going on in narrating, it is not of the events themselves, but what they mean and how we relate to them.[32]

Being able to stand back from an event and assess it from the higher-level perspective can be incredibly powerful for trauma victims. According to Goldie, appropriate emotional response is essential for closure. Goldie defines emotional closure as the ability to

> look back *in the right way* on one's past life from one's present external perspective: not just seeing the causal connections, and making sense of why one then thought, felt, and acted as one then did, but also *making an external evaluation and having emotional responses that one feels are the appropriate ones to what happened.*[33]

Though there will inevitably be interpretive issues regarding what constitutes an appropriate emotional response to any given event, a lack of what would normally be considered an appropriate emotional response or even full-blown emotional closure is perhaps most obvious in cases that involve trauma.[34]

Traumatic events can become so problematic, then, because they challenge narration in at least two ways. They are difficult to narrate because they seem to defy language, and they are also difficult to assign meaning to because they often conflict with the structures of meaning that hold up our worldview. So, while we might be able to understand the isolated traumatic event, we can have trouble when it comes to fitting it within a larger context. Or an event might feel intensely meaningful in a way that we cannot seem to narrate.

Holocaust survivor and clinician Dori Laub credits traumatic disruption to the fact that someone traumatized cannot register traumatic events properly. He explains, "Massive trauma precludes its registration; the observing and recording mechanisms of the human mind are temporarily knocked out, malfunction."[35] As discussed in chapter 2, this malfunction is a biological reality, as the presence of horror can trigger a set of responses within the nervous system that blunt access to the parts of the brain required for memory making. But perhaps it can also be understood in the sense of narrative meaning. When we feel terror, it is precisely because we cannot imagine a world in which what *is* happening could possibly *be* happening.

Laub, who works primarily with holocaust survivors, bases his clinical methods on the power of giving testimony to heal trauma. He argues that taking up the two perspectives of present and past allows for an inner dialogue that is not only necessary for integration, but also required for empathic communication within the self. The connection between the "I" and the "me"—or what Laub terms "I" and "Thou"—perspectives is essential for normal functioning. For Laub, the role of narrative is not just one of archiving, but there is always an inner dialogue occurring between these two perspectives. These two perspectives turn to one another, as it were, in order to narrate, represent, and to assign meaning to what happened. But they also turn to one another in judgment, compassion, pride, and disappointment. Think once more of Goldie's suitcase narrative. We often process what is happening (or what has happened) by way of internal dialogue. After tripping over a suitcase in the dark, one might think to oneself, "how could you be so stupid!? You know that stumbling around in the dark is bound to lead to some kind of injury!"

One of Laub's patients, a holocaust survivor whose testimony has been videotaped for the Fortunoff Video Archive for Holocaust Testimonies at Yale, describes her experience of being captured and handing her baby over to Nazi officers. As she tells the story, her eyes glaze over. She explains trying to hold the baby's mouth so it wouldn't cry, and that this eventually failed and she handed over her baby. Then she contradicts herself, claiming that it wasn't a baby that she handed over, but just a "bundle." "I think I was numb. Or something happened to me. I wasn't even there. There was no baby. I was alone with myself. Now all my life I'm alone."[36] In this woman's case, what is striking is that she acknowledges the event, and simultaneously cannot seem to let it in. She cannot forget it, but she cannot entirely remember it either. As Laub says, the victim, "'does not know' what she knows of her experience of extremity."[37] Her account is perhaps as unintelligible as the experience must feel to her. She cannot reliably occupy the "I" or the "me" perspectives enough to tell the story coherently, assign meaning to it, or even let it occupy space as a static memory.

Though victims may survive trauma physically, what has been annihilated is the inner "Thou" perspective that is necessary for internal dialogue.[38] The destruction of one half of this inner dyad is constitutive of traumatic experience, according to Laub, and healing can only happen when the dyad is restored. Restoration becomes possible when the traumatic event is narrated in the presence of another empathetic listener who can provide—from the outside—the perspective that has been annihilated. This outside perspective of the listener acts like a crutch until a conscious memory is created that can be integrated, at which point the internal dialogue is restored and the crutch is no longer needed.[39] As he explains,

> Trauma, when relived and re-experienced in the context of a dialogue with an empathic listener, may restore, to a degree, the victim's sense of being at home in the world. There is no longer the utter aloneness and incommunicability that is part of the extreme traumatic experience.[40]

We can see the relationship between narrative structure and empathetic listening if we look more closely at these perspectives within the narrative and specifically how someone else might take up a missing or fractured perspective.

INTERPERSONAL NARRATION IN THE FACE OF TRAUMA

In cases of trauma, subjects either cannot place the event in the past at all, or give a coherent narrative of what has occurred, or they can give a chronology of the events but cannot seem to respond emotionally in the right way. A crucial part of what happens is that the victim gets locked into a lower-level "me" perspective, reliving the initial event rather than being able to get any sort of distance from it. What is not available to a victim of trauma is either the ability to inhabit the higher-level perspective in a way that grants access to the emotions of the lower-level perspective in the right way, or the ability to inhabit it at all. If this higher-level perspective is not readily available to the victim, and this unavailability is a part what constitutes her trauma, one possible solution is to find a way to open it to her. This can be done through relating what happened to another person, who can embody the higher-level perspective in place of the victim, as Kardiner did in order to connect the symptoms with the trauma and help ground her in the present.[41]

By way of illustration, Goldie refers to Odysseus, who, in Book VIII of *The Odyssey*, is present at a dinner given by the king of the Phaiakians. At the dinner, the singer Demodokos entertains the guests by singing of Odysseus and his struggles. Upon hearing his own story from the perspective of another person, Odysseus weeps, understanding for the first time just how tragic his past has been. Odysseus goes on to tell his story to the guests of the party, and as he does so he begins to "evaluate and respond emotionally to his trials as he now sees that he should."[42] Witnessing another person inhabit an external perspective previously inaccessible to Odysseus makes it possible for him to experience the emotions appropriate to what he has been through. What the audience provides is a grounded external perspective through which Odysseus can come to see his experience in a new light.

Laub also argues that trauma victims need to be able to occupy both perspectives in order to survive traumatic events. As we saw above, traumatic experience interrupts this dialogue between perspectives and blocks access to the higher-level perspective that might bring coherence and empathy.

> When the empathic other totally fails in the external world of the death camps, the internal, empathic "Thou," the means for self-dialogue, ceases to exist. The ongoing internal dialogue, the internal "I" speaking to the internal "Thou," which allows for historicity, narrative, and meaning to unfold, falls silent. Sensory impressions, no matter how powerful, remain fragments that do not coalesce.[43]

Without the higher-level perspective to address and be in dialogue with, the victim is left completely alone in her trauma. She cannot provide herself the reminder of temporal distance by telling the story as something that happened in the past. Nor can she provide herself with sympathy for her experience or reactions to that experience. What the listener can provide, then, is the bridge to reestablish communication between "I" and "Thou." As Laub explains,

> In order to integrate the traumatic fragments and turn them into real knowledge, the survivor needs to locate the fervently yearned-for dialogic "Thou" within herself. She can do so by finding a trustworthy, passionate and totally present companion-listener in whom she can temporarily anchor that internal "Thou."[44]

It is crucial to note that this anchoring is *temporary*. The listener does not *become* the missing perspective any more than a crutch becomes the broken leg. Rather, through the medium of narrative and witnessing, the other person acts as a crucial part of an adaptive tool whereby the victim can gradually become to witness her own experience and provide her own grounding perspective. In other words, the third person embodies a perspective that helps re-establish the inner dialogue.

Further, it is not necessary that the perspective of the listener and that of the victim become so united that they collapse into one. Again, just as the crutch does not become the missing leg, the listener does not become the missing perspective. The embodiment of the higher-level perspective is not meant to be a replacement or an exact match, but rather a temporary approximation.

It is important to remember that the power of the higher-level perspective is not simply in its ability to establish temporal distance between the past and present, but also to provide alternative viewpoints on the emotional response that a trauma victim has to her past. In other words, the emotional closure that Goldie talks about is sometimes only possible when someone else can take up the missing perspective for the victim.

When we face trauma, shared narrative becomes a tool that is crucial for emotional closure. What narrating to others can provide in cases of trauma is an opportunity for a victim to examine her emotional response (including the meaning and coherence that she is assigning to an event) and to imagine how other perspectives might afford a different view and assessment of what happened. The power of narrative as an adaptive tool, then, lies in its ability to access an alternative higher-level perspective, assign new meaning, and find coherence in an event that seems to defy it, all the while assessing and, as appropriate, modifying the emotional import.

What we should notice in the example of Odysseus is that in the case of trauma, the perspective necessary to reevaluate emotional response and meaning is only available *interpersonally*. Odysseus could not think through the story on his own in order to gain the right perspective, he had to hear his story from someone else in order to begin to inhabit the higher-level perspective in the right way. In cases when victim reaches out for help and is rejected rather than resonated with, they become locked inside the trauma, in a never-ending loop of unbearable affect and traumatic response. This kind of response sends the message to the victim that what they have been through is *indeed* unspeakable—not in the sense of difficult to speak, but in the sense of *should not be spoken*.

THE DANGERS OF FORCING SPEECH

As mentioned above, current clinical methods relate to the power of narratives in two very different ways. Though they both focus on the necessity of narrative for healing, one forces the narrative, while a second focuses on getting the clinician to open up a space for the narrative to be created and related to. The differences in these methods are best understood through example. To do this I will turn to three brief case studies, one from my own previous research,[45] another from the memoir *The Evil Hours* by David Morris,[46] and third from Russell Carr, head of behavior health at Walter Reed hospital.

The first two involve the patient experience of Prolonged Exposure Therapy (PE), which has its roots in the Freud/Breuer abreaction/catharsis model. PE is a type of cognitive behavioral therapy in which the patient repeatedly visualizes the traumatic event and narrates that visualization in great detail in the presence of a therapist until the event loses its emotional "charge."[47] It is a method that has garnered much attention. Praise for PE in the field of psychology in general is ubiquitous. Edna Foa, credited for developing this method in the early 1980s, cites evidence-based research that "proves the efficacy of PE over other therapeutic methods."[48] It is precisely this evidence base that has been used to justify the use of this method widely and has led the US Department of Veterans Affairs to recommend it as the "gold standard" intervention for veterans with PTSD. Examining this intervention and its effects more closely allows us to see what can go wrong when we force narration in an attempt to exorcise traumatic memories.

CASE STUDY 1: DAVID MORRIS

David Morris is a reporter, writer, and former marine who participated in PE after returning from Iraq in 2013. He not only found PE to be unsuccessful but experienced a significant worsening of his symptoms. He has called PE a kind of "emotional chemo" designed to burn PTSD out of your mind and body.

He was initially open to the therapy, but as it continued, and his symptoms began to worsen, he began to see it with a different lens. As he writes:

> I began to think of the treatment not as therapy so much as punishment. Penance.
>
> It went on like this for weeks. I would show up with some things I wanted to talk about, thoughts I'd had, questions that had arisen when I looked over the journals I'd kept during the war, and after hearing me out, Scott would invariably direct me back to the imaginals. At one point, I went in and out of the cul-de-sac in Saydia eleven times in one afternoon. I say "I" went . . . because I always felt like I was alone in this activity.[49]

Imaginals are a shorthand for "imaginal exposure," a core part of PE that involves the patient repeatedly processing the traumatic memory.[50] Armed with a breathing exercise thought to promote grounding, the patient is directed to close her eyes and directly return to the painful memory and describe it as vividly as possible, using the present tense and speaking as if it were happening in the present. The therapist is instructed to monitor the patient's physiological response and to intervene when the therapist deems necessary. From behind closed lids, the patient may hear the voice of the therapist from time to time, reminding her that though she is speaking as if she were in the dangerous past, she still has one foot in the safe present. We can see why Morris felt alone. He was.

Sessions are recorded for the patient, so they can listen back at home and further process the emotions related to the event and the memory or the event. The protocol acknowledges that the process is quite unpleasant but rationalizes the discomfort in psychoeducation. This process begins with a detailed (if foreboding) explanation that this is a well-validated and successful method, and that by facing the memory in this way rather than avoiding it the patient will experience less pain in the long run.

The similarities between Freud and Breuer's abreaction/catharsis method are striking. Though the patient is not hypnotized in PE, the memory is still forced, accessed, and monitored by the clinician who steers the patient into the anxious past. When the patient wants to talk about something else, or suggest that another method may be used, they are dismissed. When Morris wanted to bring new ideas into therapy (something that would be welcomed in any other therapeutic method), he was directed again and again back to the imaginals. He quickly realized that anything other than processing singular events from deployment was beyond the scope of the method.

> This . . . was a controlled form of treatment. Scripted even. Stage-managed. I had a role to play. The role was that of the patient diligently repeating his story, *ad infinitium*. . . . It was, I would later learn, a "manualized" therapy. A therapy, in other words, whose results were designed by researchers for researchers, a therapy designed to be touted by medical administrators as being "efficacious" and scientifically tested.[51]

Rather than meet the patient in the experience, to occupy the missing perspective, clinicians watch from a distance. They are trained to direct the sessions back to the traumatic past that the patient is trying hard to avoid. When Morris tried to leave therapy, explaining that he found that the intervention was making him worse and not better, he was met with considerable resistance from his therapist. As he describes it,

> Following a heated discussion, in which I declared the therapy "insane and dangerous" and my therapist ardently defended it, we decided to call it quits. Before I left, he admonished me: "P.E. has worked for many, many people, so I would be careful about saying that it doesn't work just because it didn't work for you."[52]

Though in this case it is the patient leaving therapy, whereas Freud and Breuer abandoned their patients, it is not clear which is more destructive. It is worth spending a moment on the science that supports this method.

The idea that exposing and re-exposing patients to traumatic memories can exacerbate symptoms is well known by proponents of this method. Indeed, the method is based on scientific advancements in understanding the fear response. The basic idea is that since the fear response cannot be extinguished, it becomes activated each time the memory is relived. Revisiting it over and over again is thought to dull the fear response to the long-term benefit of the patient. Although this is undoubtedly a negative experience,

Foa and the VA hold that the therapy is still effective. Both Foa and the VA minimize possible negative effects of this method and overemphasize positive results. The VA admits that there are risks involved with PE, but they are minimal and, "most people who complete PE find that the benefits outweigh any initial discomfort."[53]

Not only has PE been shown to be effective in quantitative analysis, but there are now studies that show its efficacy visually through the use of brain imaging. For example, a study in 2016 concluded definitively that PE alters the neural circuits involved in fear extinction, correlating positively with the diminishment of PTS symptoms.

This work further strengthens the empirical evidence that supports PE, but it has serious flaws that are often not taken into account. For example, among the limitations of the 2016 study were small sample size with a *very* high attrition rate (what started out as a group with thirty participants with PTSD ended up as a group with sixteen participants) and a failure to account for differences among subgroups (e.g., male and female, combat trauma versus sexual assault, those previously traumatized versus those who were not). Despite these limitations, the report concludes, "Our findings support the idea that prolonged exposure treatment may produce a host of neural and psychophysiological changes leading to clinical improvement of PTSD."[54] What seem to be missing from this conclusion are the words, "for *some* patients." More research needs to be done to account for the incredibly high attrition rate, the conflation of types of trauma that are otherwise seen to be clinically different, and an understanding of how the patients who did not improve were affected (and potentially harmed) by the treatment.

CASE STUDY 2—JAMES

James is a former combat marine with an impressive military career who has been diagnosed with PTSD. At the time of interviewing him, he had recently completed fourteen years of active duty including multiple deployments to Iraq and Afghanistan during the course of both wars. In many ways, his career embodied the ideal for a young marine. He worked his way up to a leadership position and along the way held positions as a rifleman, team leader, squadron leader, platoon sergeant, and command sergeant. Prior to his retirement, he received multiple honors for his valor and combat exposure.

During a series of semi-structured interviews with James that took place over the course of a one-year period, something that was starkly obvious was the ways in which his treatment for PTSD failed him. Interestingly, treatment was not a failure because James's PTSD was intractable, or even because the protocol exacerbated symptoms, but because James's own experience of his PTSD and his ideas about where it originated from were completely dismissed.

Although he was living with all of the symptoms clinically associated with PTSD, the etiology of his symptoms was far from the typical conceptualization offered in a standard diagnosis of PTSD. Instead of being most effected by the violence that he saw and participated in, he was most negatively impacted by two things that are not currently captured in the clinical conception of PTSD. First, James experienced an unshakable feeling of shortcoming and failure regarding what he was able to accomplish. This feeling of shortcoming and failure was something that began in basic training and haunts him today. Second, he found that the solidarity, camaraderie, and meaning he experienced in his relationships with members of his platoon seemed to be impossible to replicate in his civilian relationships.

Right away, James had misgivings about the way that he was treated. He felt that the therapeutic environment that he was in was not equipped to understand his experience with violence, or the real etiology of his symptoms:

> When they try to treat the root problem, they focus on entirely the wrong thing, presuming that exposure to violence is what is causing the symptoms. I can tell you right now that the times that I pulled the trigger with my sights on a person, I have absolutely no issue with those experiences in any way shape, or form. I was accomplishing a mission; I was protecting me and my own and they were an evil person and the world is a better place without them. I really have no issues or qualms (with the violence). The things that bother me the most are the shots that I did not take; not the ones I did.[55]

Again, according to James's experience and contrary to a classical theoretical understanding of exposure to combat violence, he and the majority of soldiers he fought with through multiple tours of combat deployment were not necessarily averse to the combat, enemy engagement, or the violence of war. Each time that he explained this to a therapist, she dismissed his account and told him that he was incapable of understanding the source of his symptoms.

Though James felt that he had insight about his experience, he was continually met with a narrowness within the clinical setting, and he was frustrated by his therapist's inability to accept his reality—the fact that he was not averse to the violence of war. Instead, it was what James was *not* able to do in war that haunted his conscience upon leaving the theatre of war.

> I did three months of therapy (at a VA sponsored center). The head therapist started doing prolonged exposure stuff with me and I was talking about the most violent, horrific things that I had gone through. The doctor kept saying, "Why aren't you showing any emotion? You're not crying. You're not getting choked up." I said (to the doctor) *because this is not what is screwing me up*. That was

> the light bulb. I realized that this (therapy) is focused on the wrong thing. This entire treatment process is focused on the wrong thing. So if it isn't violence, what is it? Then I started thinking about what really causes me the most internal strife, anxiety, and problems. What causes me to drink? What causes me to seek out crazy behavior or anything else? It wasn't the memories of violence or anything like that. It was a need to prove myself and to accomplish a mission that I never fully could.

In a completely indirect way, narrating his experience within the PE model *did* enable James to heal. Not because it enabled him to process traumatic and violent episodes from deployment that he had yet to process, but because in its failure—in the clinician's continuous refusal to think that it might be the therapeutic *method* that was wrong, that there must be something wrong with *James*—James was able to realize what was causing him pain. Namely, the military had instilled in him an impossible mission of becoming a war hero and finishing a never-ending war. It is notable that these origins of PTSD symptoms are simply not accounted for in the clinical model.

Luckily, James is an introspective individual and he persisted down the path of his own understanding rather than cave to the clinical model that did not resonate with his experience. It is worth noting, however, that while he did this, he remained *constantly* in harm's way—suffering deeply both psychologically and physically—until he was able to sort things out on his own. He is not resentful, but he arguably has reason to be. Could he have potentially healed faster if his account was given more credibility? What further harm might he have suffered if the repeated dismissal of his own account had negatively impacted his self-esteem?

In both of these cases, we see that pushing the abreaction/catharsis model that is *still* prevalent in therapeutic contexts can sometimes work to the *detriment* of the patient, not to their benefit. A counterexample can be seen in a method that is rooted in phenomenology, rather than the abreaction/catharsis model.

CASE STUDY 3—MR. A

Russell Carr, the chair of Psychiatry at Walter Reed National Military Medical Center, uses a phenomenologically based understanding of trauma to develop short-term treatment plans for combat veterans. In a case simply titled "Mr. A in Iraq," Carr describes treatment of a soldier who had been the perpetrator of violence while deployed and was suffering from PTSD. Most notably, Mr. A suffered from persistent, vivid nightmares that were preventing him from adequate sleep.[56]

Some of the nightmares and symptoms surrounded a specific event experienced on deployment. Mr. A and his unit were on a mission to take back a village from insurgents. The village had been warned in advance and evacuated, so the unit was instructed to kill anyone that they encountered, as anyone who remained was assumed to present a significant threat. Mr. A was in charge of the machine gun on the top of one vehicle in their caravan. As they drove into town, they came across a car driving toward them. Following orders, Mr. A shot at the car. As they got closer, it became clear that the passengers were civilians. One of the three passengers was not immediately killed. He rolled out of the car, his body burning in the street. Mr. A then completed the kill by continuing to shoot the man. As the body burned, Mr. A began to smell burning flesh and started to feel hungry.

Carr discusses the way that the phenomenological viewpoint aided him in treating victims like Mr. A. Frustrated with the ineffective treatments for soldiers who were facing combat trauma, Carr came across Robert Stolorow's book *Trauma and Human Existence.* Stolorow, who is a phenomenological psychologist, defines trauma as "an experience of unbearable affect . . . constituted in an intersubjective context in which severe emotional pain cannot find a relational home in which it can be held."[57] A relational home is an intersubjective space where another person can help the individual bear those emotions and successfully put the event into the past.

On this definition, in order for someone to stop being captive of trauma so construed, that is, in order to move beyond the traumatic ground zero of unbearable pain, she must successfully adapt to it and, in keeping with Stolorow's definition, that means locating a relational home where she can gradually feel through and process (endure) the emotion with someone else. In the absence of a relational home, trauma will persist.

Reading this book helped Carr reframe his sessions with his patients and focus on "the patient's subjective experience of the recent trauma itself. . . ." For treatment, Carr began to use what he terms "empathetic introspection and the contextualization of affect."[58] By witnessing the lived experience of the individual as they recount the traumatic event and the way it made them feel, the therapist is living it *alongside of them* and providing a space in which the trauma can be relived in a more productive way. Carr explains that this may "lead the therapist into crying with the patient or offering a hand to hold as they *bear the pain together.*"[59] In this experience, the unbearable emotion finds a relational home in the empathetic reaction of the therapist. The traumatic event, when borne by another individual, can stop being isolating and purely bodied. It can then gradually be named, understood, and placed in the past so that the symptoms slowly diminish. When successful, this helps integrate the emotional experience of trauma into the horizon of the individual so that they can continue interacting with the world similar to the way they did before the trauma. What is distinctly phenomenological about this approach is that it is based on the idea that understanding and empathizing with the lived experience (rather than simply directing the repetition of it) is central to healing. This is distinct from PE because it is grounded in the clinician *feeling with* the patient, rather than just listening in while the patient—with closed eyes—travels back into the past alone.

Carr writes of Mr. A's eventual confession, "It was his horror at himself for becoming so savage that Mr. A wanted to confess. Instead of violating the laws of armed conflict, he seemed to fear that he had violated the laws of being human."[60] In other words, it wasn't simply what happened to Mr. A, but what *it meant*; how that event might color the story one might tell about Mr. A, or the story he might tell about himself. How could it possibly be true, given the narrative that Mr. A had been living, that he would feel hungry at the smell of the burning human flesh of a civilian that he killed? How could he tell this story to himself or loved ones? What does it tell about who he is if the smell of burning human flesh made him hungry? At the center of this trauma for Mr. A is the inability to reconcile what happened with what he previously thought of himself and of the world. An essential part of what caused Mr. A to experience symptoms of PTSD is *not* simply that he experienced a deeply upsetting event, but what that event *meant*.

In this case, it is apparent that what narrative has done is precisely to help Mr. A gain a different perspective on what happened and to reassess his original emotional response. He came into therapy with one perspective on the event in Iraq—he was a person who murdered civilians and then became hungry at the smell of their burning, human flesh and this meant that he could be tried for war crimes, that he violated the laws of human decency, that he is a monster. The emotional response that he had was marked by guilt, fear, and horror; instead of closure, Mr. A repeatedly relived the initial event from the lower-level perspective in dreams and flashbacks. In this case, Mr. A could tell the story of the traumatic event, but he could not gain a perspective that allowed him to assess his emotional response to that event.

In narrating the story and talking about what that story meant to him, Mr. A was then given access to an alternative higher-level perspective through Carr's response to his story. Carr's emotional response was not one of disgust, but one of empathy. He felt that what Mr. A had been through was horrible, that anyone might have had the same reaction, and that he hadn't violated any laws of war or human decency. In narrating the story alongside someone who was able to embody an alternative higher-level perspective for him, Mr. A finally became able to stand back from his singular non-empathetic perspective. His dialogue with Carr allowed Mr. A to step into a new higher-level perspective and jettison his previous sense of meaning for a new one, which marked the lessening of his PTSD symptoms. Though PE involves processing emotions related to the trauma, it does not engage with meaning in the way that Carr's phenomenological method does.

When looking at these three case studies side by side, we can see that though they each have their origin in the idea that narrative is central to both traumatic experience and healing from trauma, the way that that narrative is approached makes a great deal of difference. Picking up threads set down by Freud and Breuer leads to the deployment of a therapy that, at best, does not work very well, and, at worst, actively makes patients worse. Picking up threads set down by Kardiner, on the other hand, leads to a phenomenological approach wherein the clinician meets the patient in their pain and anxiety and leads them to empathy and peace.

CONCLUSION

When it comes to narrating traumatic events, clinical methods have evolved from simply understanding and cataloguing symptoms to focusing on the inner conscious experience of the traumatized patient and encouraging adaptation there. Phenomenology is crucial to this piece in particular. As Laub acknowledges,

> While both [psychoanalytic and neuroscientific] approaches offer a general understanding of the psychological phenomenology of extreme traumatic experience, neither specifically examines this phenomenology in order to glean from it a more precise understanding of its unique experiential dimension. Both stop short of looking at such experience from "the inside."[61]

Though it may seem a minor distinction, when we look from above rather than from the inside, understanding and relating to someone else's trauma is nearly impossible. To be sure, there is no clinical method that works for every patient. Human psychology is simply too complex for that to be true. What we see here, though, is a compelling argument that the creation of a relational home is necessary for healing from trauma, and also that one of the most widely used methods of treating combat trauma fails to do that. We have a responsibility to look critically at the clinical methods we employ to ensure that we are not doing more damage than good. Or, arguably, to ensure that we are not doing any damage at all.

What is especially chilling about reading the accounts from Morris and James is that though they survived, they did so through a mix of tenacity and good luck. There is a deep-rooted assumption that the suicide statistics can be blamed on combat trauma alone. What if some of the blood is on our hands too?

NOTES

1. For an excellent article on the benefits that the phenomenological viewpoint can bring to psychology, see Kevin Aho, "Medicalizing Mental Health: A Phenomenological Alternative," *Journal of Medical Humanities* 29, no. 4 (2008): 243–259.

2. Freud and Breuer, *Studies on Hysteria*, 37–38.

3. Ibid., 40–41, emphasis added.

4. Anna O. was a pseudonym for Bertha Pappenheim. There are two things that are especially important to note about her case. First, though the case study in *Studies on Hysteria* states that Anna O. was cured, this was not the case. After treating her for about two years, Breuer admitted her to Bellevue Sanatorium (which was under the direction of Ludwig Biswanger), where she remained suffering for several years. Pappenheim eventually recovered and became an influential scholar and feminist. The second thing that is important to note is that her case is cited as the beginning of what would come to be called the "talking cure." For the importance of Anna O. in the early days of psychoanalysis, see Dianne Hunter, "Hysteria, Psychoanalysis, and Feminism: The Case of Anna O.," *Feminist Studies* 9, no. 3 (1983): 464–488. In many ways, the case studies presented in *Studies on Hysteria* can be seen as the beginning of psychoanalysis. See also Herman, *Trauma and Recovery*, 19–20. For a thorough exploration of her life and mental illness, see Mikkel Borch-Jacobsen, *Remembering Anna O.: A Century of Mystification* (New York: Routledge, 1996).

5. Freud and Breuer, *Studies on Hysteria*, 56.

6. Ibid., 67.

7. Ibid., 69.

8. Ibid., 70. This moment in this particular case study marks the birth of the term "talking cure."

9. Ibid., 43.

10. Though the ideas of abreaction and catharsis are repeated throughout the case studies in *Studies on Hysteria*, they are first mentioned in the Preliminary Communications on page 43.

11. Kardiner, *Traumatic Neuroses of War*, 216.

12. Ibid., 216–232.

13. Ibid., 227.

14. Ibid., 222.

15. Ibid., 223.

16. Ibid., 223.

17. Ibid., 220.

18. Kardiner, *Traumatic Neuroses of War*, 74. Even within Kardiner's definition of trauma, we can again see a turn toward a phenomenological understanding of trauma. This language of trauma, injury, and adaptation would be used by Merleau-Ponty just five years later in his attempt to give a phenomenological account of Schneider's combat trauma.

19. Ibid., 226.

20. Alphons Richert, *Integrating Existential and Narrative Therapy* (Pittsburgh: Duquesne University Press, 2010), 28–35.

21. For an excellent account of the influence of narrative therapy as well as an understanding of the ways in which this method is grounded in philosophy, see A. C. (Tina) Besley, "Foucault and the Turn to Narrative Therapy," *British Journal of Guidance and Counselling* 30, no. 2 (2002): 125–143. See also Alan Carr, "Michael White's Narrative Therapy," *Contemporary Family Therapy* 20, no. 4 (1998): 485–503.

22. Michael White and David Epston, *Narrative Means to Therapeutic Ends* (New York: W.W. Norton & Company, 1990), 1–13.

23. Richert, *Integrative Existential and Narrative Therapy,* 80–104.

24. See, for example, Eugene Gendlin, *Experiencing and the Creation of Meaning: A Philosophical and Psychological Approach to the Subjective* (New York: Free Press of Glencoa, 1962). For an excellent summary of the felt-implicit as it relates to the clinical use of narrative, see, Richert, *Integrating Existential and Narrative Therapy*, 26–27 & 44.

25. It should be noted here that Goldie writes more often about grief than trauma. He does briefly discuss the importance of emotional closure and trauma, and many of his examples (discussed below) refer to a kind of traumatic loss. For these reasons, I think it is uncontroversial to imagine that he would be sympathetic to my claims about narrative and trauma here.

26. Peter Goldie, *The Mess Inside: Narrative, Emotion, and the Mind* (New York: Oxford University Press, 2012), 2.

27. Peter Goldie, "One's Remembered Past: Narrative Thinking, Emotion, and the External Perspective," *Philosophical Papers* 32, no. 3 (2003): 304–305.

28. Peter Goldie, "Narrative and Perspective; Values and Appropriate Emotions," in *Philosophy and the Emotions*, ed. Anthony Hatzimoysis (New York: Cambridge University Press, 2003), 206.

29. It is important to note that though the language of perspectives here invokes spatial relationships, the internal and external perspectives that Goldie describes are temporal. The internal perspective is inside the event and the external perspective is outside, allowing us to occupy the present as we describe the past, for example.

30. Goldie, "Narrative and Perspective," 206.

31. Goldie is aware that that the objectivity available in the higher-level perspective is not objective in the strictest sense of the word, because any narrative is first personal. However, he argues that just because a narrative is subjective, it does not follow that it is not objective in any sense. See Goldie, *The Mess Inside*, Chapter 7 for a thorough discussion on narrative and truth.

32. There is always a kind of tension in narrative between the story being told about the event and the event itself. Questions of the extent to which the narrative can accurately represent what happened naturally arise. In my own definition of narrative above, I highlight the importance of understanding the narration to be both beholden to objective reality in some sense, but at the same time always articulating a particular subjective perspective. I maintain, following Goldie, that the perspective from which the narrative is being told does not necessarily falsify the event.

33. Goldie, *The Mess Inside*, 71, emphasis added.

34. Ibid., 70–75.

35. Shoshana Felman and Dori Laub, *Testimony: Crises of Witnessing in Literature, Psychoanalysis, and History* (New York: Routledge, 1991), 57.
36. Testimony from Bessie K. in the film *Witness* (New Haven, CT: Yale University, 1987), Yale Fortunoff Video Archive, http://www.library.yale.edu/testimonies/publications/witness.html. A partial transcript of this testimony also appears in Dori Laub, "Reestablishing the Internal 'Thou' in Testimony of Trauma," *Psychoanalysis, Culture & Society* 18, no. 2 (2013): 192–193.
37. Laub, "Reestablishing the Internal 'Thou,'" 184–198.
38. Ibid., 184.
39. Ibid., 187.
40. Ibid., 196.
41. Ibid., 72.
42. Ibid., 73.
43. Ibid., 188.
44. Ibid.
45. Gary Senecal and MaryCatherine McDonald, "Mission Completion, Troop Welfare, and Destructive Idealism," *New Male Studies: An International Journal* 6, no. 2 (2017): 64–89.
46. Morris, *The Evil Hours*.
47. It should be noted that Prolonged Exposure Therapy (PE) is not the same thing as Narrative Exposure Therapy (NE). Narrative Exposure Therapy is a more recently developed therapeutic method that focuses on integrating traumatic events into the life story of the patient. Since PE involves the repeated narration of the specific traumatic memory, it seems to align more closely with Freud and Breuer's abreaction/catharsis model.
48. Edna Foa, E. Hembree, and B. Rothbaum, *Prolonged Exposure Therapy for PTSD: Emotional Processing of Traumatic Experiences: Therapist Guide* (New York: Oxford University Press, 2007). Edna Foa, T. Keane, and M. Friedman, *Effective Treatments for PTSD* (New York: Guilford, 2010).
49. Morris, *The Evil Hours*, 181.
50. The second pillar of PE is a process called "in vivo" in which the patient confronts situations that they are consciously avoiding in their everyday life. Since much of this work happens outside of the session, I focus here on imaginals.
51. Morris, *The Evil Hours*, 181.
52. David Morris, "After PTSD, More Trauma," *New York Times* (New York, NY), January 17, 2015.
53. "Prolonged Exposure Therapy for PTSD," United States Department of Veterans Affairs, accessed August 24, 2018. https://www.ptsd.va.gov/public/treatment/therapy-med/prolonged-exposure-therapy.asp.
54. Liat Helpman, et al., "Neural Changes in Extinction Recall Following Prolonged Exposure Treatment for PTSD: A Longitudinal fMRI Study," *Neuroimage: Clinical* 12 (2016): 715–723.
55. The qualitative data cited here were obtained in compliance with all IRB protocol and were approved by Institutional Review Boards at College of the Holy Cross and Old Dominion University.

56. Carr, "Combat and Human Existence," 1–26. It should be noted that this is not an exhaustive account of this case study, which also includes other traumatic experiences and symptoms.
57. Robert Stolorow, *Trauma and Human Existence: Autobiographical, Psychoanalytic, and Philosophical Reflections* (New York: Analytic, 2007).
58. Carr, "Combat and Human Existence," 3–4.
59. Ibid., 18, emphasis added.
60. Carr, "Combat and Human Existence," 14.
61. Ibid., 197.

Chapter 5

Haunted by a Different Ghost

The word "haunted" can be traced back to Old Norse *heimta*, which means "to bring home." Often when we think about being haunted, we imagine being tortured from without by some random and terrifying external thing. Perhaps this is not quite right. Perhaps instead we are haunted in part by *what we bring in*. That our ghosts are constituted from the inside out, rather than the other way around. Our ghosts—what we are haunted by—must then be as varied as we are. If our lives and our bodies and our horizons are stamped with our experiences and what they mean to us, there are perhaps an infinite number of ways to be haunted, an infinite number of kinds of ghosts to bring home.

When we think about the haunted veteran, we imagine that the ghost is always the same. The ghost is the face of the civilian that he killed or the bloodied body of the comrade he could not save. But there are many different kinds of ghosts. One may be haunted by things that seem more benign—stray puppies in Vietnam, the sound of helicopter wings, the specific color red of the wire sticking out of the IED (Improvised Explosive Device) just before it got tripped, the haze and heat of the desert, or as in the case of my father, the sound of cockroaches scattering when he flipped on the light in the middle of the night.

Perhaps the worst kinds of ghosts are those that are less specific, less traceable—the memory of the vague feeling of unease on the morning of a mission that turned out badly (*was* that feeling there that morning, or is it a figment of hindsight?); the tiny realization that just appears one day and reveals that though war is *here* and *not home*, that it is also everywhere, unshakable; the sick and dark humor that saves you and keeps you sane but also signals that the world—in total—might *just not make any sense*; the knowledge that though you can go home (hopefully), that in some sense you can also never go home.

The point is that veterans are sometimes haunted in unexpected ways, and if we miss this, we miss the opportunity to exorcise those ghosts. Veterans are haunted in ways that are hard to outline and understand, hard to defend oneself against, and hard to even discover. In the previous chapter, we see that James, for example, was not at all haunted by the violence he had perpetrated, but by the aching and unrelenting feeling that he had had set off for a mission that could never be completed. Mr. A was haunted by the violence that he perpetrated, but not in the sense we might expect. It was not what he had done that haunted him, but the way that his body instinctively responded to the gruesomeness of war.

As we saw in chapter 2, being haunted is at the center of trauma. Symptoms of reliving—bringing home the ghosts who then take hold of the present in the form of memories and nightmares—are arguably the focal point of PTSD. In this chapter, I want to explore the ways in which veterans might be haunted unexpectedly—by ghosts that we have so far been unaware of. We miss this because of our tendency toward reductionism, which then influences our expectations of trauma. Though it is certainly true that they are sometimes haunted in the ways that we've predicted (specific memories of violence, witnessed or perpetrated), *what if the key is that veterans are also haunted by a different kind of ghost?* A ghost that has to do with the crumbling of one's moral structures, of the potential meaninglessness of the world, rather than what one has done or seen.

Though this may sound ephemeral and vague, it is actually quite stark and specific. When we reduce our understanding of a phenomena to singular explanations, we risk missing alternate sources of suffering. When we miss sources of suffering, we also risk lives. Because this is what is so terrifying about being haunted—when it gets bad enough, one will do *anything* to make it stop. It is not always survivor's guilt, anxiety, or depression that is at the root of suicide. Sometimes it is simply *unbearability*.

I will start here, with the idea of suicide having its roots in desperation and not depression. Then I will turn to examine some of the ways in which we fail our veterans, by failing to recognize just how they are haunted. As the suicide statistics that this book began with reveal, this is a matter of life and death.

SUICIDE AND WHAT WAR REVEALS

Primo Levi is perhaps most famous not for what he did while he was here (he was a holocaust survivor, a chemist, husband and father, and a *prolific* writer), but for the way he went out. Forty years after surviving Auschwitz, he committed suicide in a way that seemed so mundane and senseless that people still argue that it must have been an accident. He woke up, went about his regular morning routine, picked up his mail, and then leapt to his death in the stairwell of his apartment building. It is not that he committed suicide that is so striking, but *when*. That Levi had survived for so long makes the act seem inexplicable. Why forty years later and not sooner? Why after forty years of successful survival, of struggling to heal, was suicide appealing? How does Levi's suicide reflect back onto his life? Does it mean that he did not really heal from his trauma? Even in death his life seems to lie in limbo—he exists in between surviving and not surviving—and this is not something that we can easily understand.

A part of our failure to understand lies in the fact that our assumptions about what it is like to suffer from trauma are based on fairly narrow stereotypes. Here they are polarized. We believe that one *either* survives or does not. That either one survives and walks into the light, following a neat and linear path of healing, or that one cannot bear it and upon this realization, immediately becomes suicidal. Though we may want them to, our actions do not always track into coherence so neatly.

Perhaps a part of the answer lies precisely in the temporality of Levi's suicide in that forty-year delay. There are two things that are behind that delay. The first has to do with weight over time. As we have seen, trauma carries with it a weight, it is a burden. When it comes to physical weight, we easily see that what is not *inherently* heavy (a two-pound weight, for example) can *become* very heavy the longer one is tasked with holding it up. Why would we assume it would be any different with psychological weight? What was bearable can become increasingly unbearable over time. The second thing that belies the delay has to do with the narrowness with which we understand healing. First, we assume that *because* Levi wrote—and that he wrote specifically about his trauma—that all of his ghosts were exorcized. They must have been—he wrote his story, proving that he has healed. Relatedly, we assume that *because* he wrote, he (and by extension his audience) knew exactly what shape his ghosts took. That they were discoverable, intelligible, and traceable; they could be addressed and understood and accordingly sent away.

When we assume that success involves being able to put down the past, and that when it is completed it is completed, we forget the fact that because the past is so ephemeral, because we carry it with us and bring it home, there are pieces of it that *never completely recede*. These pieces themselves might not be that heavy, but when we hold onto them for forty years, they *become heavy*. Levi's suicide is conceptually problematic only when we try to craft it into the tidy narrative wherein people either survive or they do not.

After his suicide, amidst all of the speculation and discussion about it, Levi's son Renzo pointed to the conclusion of Levi's *The Reawakening* for explanation. The conclusion reads:

> [And] a dream full of horror has still not ceased to visit me, at sometimes frequent, sometimes longer, intervals. It is a dream within a dream, varied in detail, one in substance. I am sitting at a table with my family, or with friends, or at work, or in the green countryside; in short, in a peaceful relaxed environment, apparently without tension or affliction; yet I feel a deep and subtle anguish, the definite sensation of an impending threat. And in fact, as the dream proceeds, slowly and brutally, each time in a different way, everything collapses, and disintegrates around me, the scenery, the walls, the people, while the anguish becomes more intense and more precise. Now everything has changed into chaos; I am alone in the centre of a grey and turbid nothing, and now, I know what this thing means, and I also know that I have always known it; I am in the Lager once more, and nothing is true outside the Lager. All the rest was a brief pause, a deception of the senses, a dream; my family, nature in flower, my home. Now this inner dream, this dream of peace, is over, and in the outer dream, which continues, gelid, a well-known voice resounds: a single word, not imperious, but brief and subdued. It is the dawn command, of Auschwitz, a foreign word, feared and expected: get up, *"Wstawàch"*.[1]

The ghost that Levi is haunted by here is the specter of a world without meaning—of a world that fundamentally contains evil within it; this particular ghost is relentless, nonspecific, horrifying. What we see in this passage is that Levi was haunted not only by his experience at Auschwitz but by *what that experience revealed about the world*—namely, that there was no meaning that could contain such evil within it. We can also see the unbearable contradiction of life after trauma which shatters the narrative that one either gets over it or one does not. Instead, life is livable *and* it is not. One survives *and* one does not.

Though life *was* livable after the holocaust, perhaps the small contentment and peace that Levi did get in surviving was *not* enough to rewrite (or re-right) Levi's universe. Perhaps the trauma of the holocaust did more than stamp Levi's life with meaning, its ink spilled onto and into *everything*. Once the terrible truth of evil in the world was revealed to Levi in Auschwitz, peace after that was impossible. Peace could only be temporary, a dream to be woken up from—back into the nightmare of reality. Sometimes trauma peels back all that is good and cheery about the world and reveals a dark and swirling abyss underneath. So even in light of signposts that suggest survival—success, productivity, what looks like peace—at some point, the only thing left is to say, "Enough. I have had enough."

The prevailing societal narrative about suicide (and for good reason) is that it has its root in depression. That one reaches a point at which there is no more hope, no point, no nothing—and that it is because one can no longer think of a good reason to continue to live that one chooses to die. Though this is certainly the case some of the time, not all suicides fit that mold.

Indeed, veteran suicide in particular seems distinct in some ways. Though depression certainly may be at their root in some cases, other cases have their source in a desperate need to escape—to get away from that which is ceaselessly, relentlessly haunting you. I bring up Primo Levi here specifically not simply because he suffered trauma and committed suicide, but because of the delay and what it suggests. Though in the absence of a suicide note we can only speculate as to the reason Levi committed suicide, perhaps what the delay suggests is that at the root of some post-trauma suicide is *desperation* rather than *depression*, a need to stop reality—anxiety that tips into unbearability rather than melancholy. Perhaps the delay suggests that even when one looks successful, and achieves some measure of success, this does not mean that they have stopped being haunted.

It is worth saying this: we cannot save every veteran (or every person) from suicide. Nor should we. The end of suffering can be a merciful thing. It is critical to understand the extent and relentlessness of unbearable experience. As William Styron writes, "To the tragic legion who are compelled to destroy themselves there should be no more reproof attached than to the victims of terminal cancer."[2]

That being said, it is certainly still worth investigating how we can improve the lives of our veterans. Though the statistics are incomplete, it is estimated that the risk for suicide for the veteran population is 22 percent higher than the rest of the population in the United States alone. Using the framework from the book thus far, I want to suggest that we exacerbate the problem first by misunderstanding the way that they are haunted and second by failing to provide them with relational homes in which to cope with what they bring home. I worry that it is this—at least in part—that makes suicide in general (and perhaps suicide on a delay) more likely.

MISUNDERSTANDING THE GHOST

In order to understand what the ghosts look like, it is necessary to revisit the phenomenological idea of meaning. If the ghosts are things that *we bring in*, it follows that they are constituted (at least partially) by the meaning we assign to our experiences, consciously or less so. So what is *meaning*, exactly? And where does it come from?

In his book *A Leg to Stand On*, neurologist Oliver Sacks describes his experience of encountering a bull while hiking alone in Norway. When he first saw the bull, he tried to keep his composure and calmly walk away, but fear took over and he started running down the mountain, only stopping because he fell and suffered a catastrophic break in his leg. He immediately switched into examining doctor mode and attempts to comprehend the extent of the break.

> "Ok, doctor," I said to myself, "would you kindly examine the leg?"
>
> Very professionally, and impersonally, and not at all tenderly, as if I were a surgeon examining a "case," I took the leg and examined it—feeling it, moving it this way and that. I murmured my findings aloud as I did so, as if for a class of students.
>
> I turned with a pleased smile to my invisible audience, as if awaiting a round of applause. And then suddenly, the "professional" attitude and *persona* broke down, and I realized that this fascinating case was *me—me, myself*, fearfully disabled, and quite likely to die.[3]

When we are physically injured, we look for the edges of the injury, in an attempt to understand the extent of it so that we can begin the work of adaptation. What we are looking for is not just biological reality but *meaning*. The question is not just, "Is this a hairline fracture or a break?" It is also, "What does this injury mean for me? How will I get to work with a cast on my right leg? How will this change my life and the way I am in the world?" In Sacks's case, what was especially terrifying was that he was *alone*, and he knew that his aloneness would mark his demise. This is metaphorical. With both physical and psychological trauma, we might be able to determine the extent of the damage ourselves, but we can seldom do the work of healing alone.

In fact, meaning is never created alone. A natural extension of the argument that we are embodied beings-in-the-world (and not just minds with bodies) is that we are always embedded in a social world. A part of our horizon or milieu and the meaning that it contains, then, is socially constructed. Meaning is not a completely autonomous value—decided on freely by the individual from an infinite set of possible meanings. What a traumatic injury *means* to the survivor, then, is partially given over to her social environment.

For example, what it means to be a survivor of sexual assault is related to the value placed on sexuality in that culture. In cultures where virginity is seen as a sacred value for the woman and the family she belongs to, women can be sentenced to death for *being* raped (e.g., honor killings). The significance of that experience is different in that culture than it is in cultures that do not view virginity in this way or do not participate in honor killings. Meaning also shifts through time as cultural values shift. In the United States, marital rape was not considered a crime until the early 1970s. What it meant to be raped by one's spouse in the 1950s is different than what it means today. This does not mean that these experiences are or are not inherently traumatic, but that the meaning of the trauma is always multifaceted, prismatic. What it *means* to be traumatized—the significance it has, the way it is processed, how it is mapped on to personal identity—is both socially and personally constructed.

All of this is to say that our working definition of meaning might be this: the significance (importance, gravity, import, implication) of an event, and the significance of that event is constituted by both personal and social values.

Despite the fact that meaning is embedded in both personal and societal structures that are difficult to trace and reduce, we nevertheless tend to stereotype experience, assuming that there is something specific and singular about what it is like to be a veteran, and by extension that there is something specific and singular about what it means to be a traumatized veteran. While it is certainly important to notice *trends* in experience, when the trends tilt into reductive stereotypes, they can create barriers to understanding.

The most common stereotype of the veteran is as follows. He is hypervigilant and paranoid and hits the floor anytime he hears a loud noise. He is haunted by who he has lost or what he has seen, and as a result, he is fragile and scared and his behavior is erratic and he needs to be treated with kid gloves.

This stereotype—which is sometimes accurate—is problematic for two reasons. First, when we reduce experience to singular understandings we risk missing important pieces of the experience. If this is the only way to be a traumatized veteran according to the social script, then veterans who *are* traumatized but whose trauma *does not look like this* have no place.

It is also destructive because of the way the stereotype gets deployed. We do not use this stereotype to empathize with this person, to anticipate his needs, or to ensure that his right to mental health care is protected. We talk about it because we are fascinated by it—and a little bit scared. Is this person our neighbor? A co-worker? Is he pacing again? Does he have a gun? Should we call the police? We stereotype those who are traumatized as weak, broken, and overcome by fear and their emotions if not directly, then certainly by suggestion. This stereotype is loaded with judgment. The implication is that those who come home from war without PTSD are heroic—stronger and more capable—than those who come home from war traumatized. One can almost hear the echoes of Yealland here: "You didn't behave like the hero I expected you to be."[4]

This stereotyping happens from inside the population, as well as from without. A recent—and quite vivid—example can be seen in the trauma that plagues drone operators. This example is especially useful because in it we can see how the stereotyping of combat veterans can come from a number of different sources.

Briefly, the military has been using unmanned aerial vehicles (UAVs), more typically referred to as drones, since 2014. Their entrance into warfare was swift; in Operation Iraqi Freedom and Operation Enduring Freedom alone, drones flew over 100,000 flight hours. Sometimes the drones are used to simply collect data—flying over large swaths of land and taking photos and videos. Other times, they have a much more active role, as they are used to kill what are called "high value targets" from the sky.

In some ways, this technology might be thought as something that would likely reduce the chances of trauma for soldiers who use them. It makes it possible to explore, and fight (and kill) from a distance of safety, removing the feeling of threat from combat. Unfortunately, it seems that rather than reducing combat trauma in general, drone combat has created a new way of being traumatized. One of the contributing factors of what has been termed "drone trauma" is that it challenges our narrative about what it means to fight. We can see this in the following report by drone pilot Brandon Bryant:

> It was horrifying to know how easy it was. I felt like a coward because I was halfway around the world and the guy never even knew I was there. I felt like I was haunted by a legion of the dead. My physical health was gone, my mental health crumbled. . . . When you are exposed to it over and over again it becomes like a small video, embedded in your head, forever on repeat, causing psychological pain and suffering that many people will hopefully never experience.[5]

It seems that there are two relevant aspects to this kind of combat that make it especially traumatic. The first sentence in this passage speaks to the norms that we insert into combat experience. Namely, killing someone *should not be too easy*. War is about strength, struggle, and danger. If it is too easy, the act of killing no longer fits within the archetype. The archetype of the soldier who kills tells of a stoic character that participates in real (not virtual) violence which requires the strength and struggle of his body, and then later on he is tragically haunted by what he has done. Though drone killing may be horrifying in many ways, it is worth noting that a part of the horror relates to the disconnect between the expectation/archetype of combat and the reality of it.

In the example of drone combat, we see that this kind of stereotyping of experience extends all the way into the temporality of combat and trauma. There is an expected temporal narrative arc to being traumatized. First, one valiantly does what one has to do on the battlefield, and then later (not too much later, but enough later), one feels guilty about it and is haunted by what one has seen or done, and these hauntings take over memory and dreams. In drone warfare, the temporality of this narrative collapses. The traumatic symptom that haunts the memory of the veteran—seeing the experience over and over again on a screen—literally happens *at the time of the event*. The traumatic symptom that is supposed to come much later is present immediately. Being so quickly haunted is not something that we are as prepared to understand because it does not square with the narrative arc that we subscribe to.

Given how much the drone format challenges our typical understanding of combat, it is perhaps unsurprising that being a traumatized drone pilot is highly stigmatized even *within* the military. How can you be traumatized when your life wasn't in danger? How can you be traumatized by what is essentially a really realistic version of a video game? There is also the idea that without threat of actual physical harm, one cannot be traumatized (indeed, this is stipulated in the first criteria for PTSD in the DSM). If fighting from behind a screen is so much safer, what is there to be traumatized by, exactly? When discussing drone trauma with a veteran (who was otherwise compassionate and kind), he angrily drew a thick, black line in the sand, saying, "those guys don't even know what it's like. They haven't even seen combat. It's just ridiculous. They sat behind a goddamned desk." Resentment and comparison, validated by stereotypes about combat, make compassion and empathy impossible.

This example shows just how destructive and isolating these societal stereotypes can be. In a number of ways, because of this impulse to categorize experience in singular ways, we fail to provide an outlet for the veteran to process and bear this pain. How is one supposed to even begin to heal when one's wound is not recognized? When the experienced is not recognized as traumatic (neither by society nor by one's peers) to begin with? There is also self-shame here. Amidst this stigma, how can the drone pilot square his experience with the experience of his fellow soldiers—some of whom fought in the battlefield, participated in and witnessed atrocities and did *not* end up with PTSD?

The example of drone trauma serves as a microcosm of combat trauma in general. What this example reveals is that the stereotyping of combat (and combat trauma) doesn't just prevent us from understanding it fully, it also leads to the creation of a hierarchy of trauma wherein there are certain kinds of experience (being seriously wounded, witnessing the brutal death of a fellow soldier) that count as potentially traumatic, and other kinds of experience (being wounded in a more minor way, killing from behind a drone camera) do not count. This hierarchy appears both within military culture and culture at large, and it is destructive for both groups—those who experience that which we expect to be traumatic are assumed to have PTSD even when they do not, and those who experience that which we do not expect to be traumatic have no safe place to lay down their burden.

To return to meaning, and to being haunted, the emphasis on meaning in perception can help us crack through the stereotypical categories and get to the center of the experience. When we focus on what the experience means to the individual who is experiencing it—rather than trying to find the generalizable explanation that matches—we see that the injury is not limited to the singular event, but that it extends out to their perceptual world at large. *The world as they experience it in general has been stamped with the meaning that the injury carries with it.* So though the traumatized may be haunted by specific ghosts (remnants of the past), the ghost that we have missed is the one that heralds a world with no meaning.

WAR AND WORLDS WITHOUT MEANING

In order to give some shape to these shadowy figures, I want to turn to five different accounts from veterans. What they each have in common is a shattering of structures of meaning in general. It seems that something that is occurring in war trauma but is unaccounted for in the clinical understanding is that war—in all of its paradoxes, sacrifices, losses—challenges the combat veteran's idea that there is *any* sort of structure of meaning that holds at all.

In the following account, one of Jonathan Shay's patients, a veteran from Vietnam, describes a situation in which he witnessed the death of a fellow combat soldier.

> When you jump off a tank, we were always taught to jump off the right front fender. And that's exactly where I jumped. I jumped off and started clearing away some brush and shit, and going to put up the lean-to. And I started doing it.
>
> And [he] yells down, he says, "I'll do it. Get that fucking pep–." I had pepperoni, cans of raviolis, that's what I can remember. I had other stuff, I don't know what the hell it was. But I remember the pepperoni had all white furry stuff on it from the heat. I got back up. I got back on, on the right side in the back sprocket, y'know, crawled to the back, so the turret's in front. And the turret's here, and here's my package. So I opened the package.
>
> And [he]'s probably fifteen feet away. And when he jumped, he jumped . . . ah-WHUH. . . . He jumped on a mine.
>
> And there was nothing left of him.
>
> He wasn't a harmful person. He wasn't a dirty person. He had this head that was wide up at the top, and his chin come down to a point. He had this hair he used to comb to his right side, and he always had this big cowlick in back. Big old cowlick. And when he smiled—you ever hear "ear to ear"?—it was almost a gooney-looking smile. You know, it was just wa-a-ay—it was huge. He just had this big, huge smile. He never said nothing bad about nobody. He was just . . . he was a caring person.
>
> And when you're on a tank, it's like a closeness you never had before. It's closer than your mother or father, closest than your brother or sister, or whoever you're closest with in your family. . . . Because you get three guys that are on that tank, and you're just stuck together. You're there.
>
> It should've been me.
>
> I jumped first. It didn't blow me up. Sa-a-ame spot. Same spot. Same exact spot.[6]

In a world where structures of justice hold—where goodness is rewarded and evil punished—this situation sticks out because it is senseless. It does not fit the mold of right and wrong and *this* is why it remains present for the veteran. This is why it is so traumatic, because it shatters those structures of justice. Nancy Sherman aptly calls this "moral dislocation," suggesting that in these cases, one's moral foundation has been disturbed or fractured. Something essential has been displaced and won't right itself.[7]

We can hear this in the veteran's account: his explanation of the sequence of events is inextricably tied to the character of the victim. The victim "wasn't a harmful person. He wasn't a dirty person." He had endearing qualities and a great big smile. The veteran is not simply describing his friend; he is attempting to make sense out of the senseless. The implication is that if he were a harmful person, if he were a dirty person, if he didn't have any endearing qualities, maybe the death would have made sense. What is most relevant here is what the event signifies—which is that the structures of belief that previously held up and organized the world collapse. This one episode is so upsetting because of the meaning that it stamps on the world—or, perhaps more accurately, the meaning that it stamps out.

Under the current conceptualizations of combat trauma, what this veteran is expressing would most likely be considered a pretty straightforward case of survivor's guilt. He even directly says toward the end of his account, "It should have been me." While that is undoubtedly *a part* of what is going on here, guilt at surviving does not capture the entire phenomenon. This is not simply a matter of getting this veteran to forgive himself for living, for having the audacity to jump on the trigger and somehow not trigger the bomb. In fact, due to the senseless nature of this "crime" of survival, forgiveness seems impossible. How can one be forgiven for something so arbitrary?

It might be the case that in part, guilt is a lesser of two evils, a kind of coping mechanism. If blame can be found, one still has to mourn the loss but the world remains intact. If there is blame, one does not have to come to grips with a world in which senseless death occurs. What we see in this account is that the perceptual horizon of this veteran has been stamped with the meaning of that event. Again, this meaning is not limited to that particular moment or to that loss. Rather, it challenges the very structures of morality and moral order that previously held true.

When a veteran is grappling with trauma, then, it is not simply a matter of getting her to forgive herself. Even if that is helpful or necessary to alleviate some of the symptoms, it does not treat the underlying problem, which is that *the set of beliefs that she once relied on are gone*. The phenomenological perspective reminds us that the experience has *altered the fabric of her horizon altogether*; it is not just this particular instance of guilt that is a problem, but the very way that she perceives the world.

For further evidence that illustrates the global loss of a sense of moral structure, I will now turn to qualitative interviews with veterans that have been completed over the past year during research on the complexities of veteran reintegration.[8] Similar issues relating to moral dislocation come up again and again.

Participant A: I want to but I don't know how to say it. . . . The biggest change is that I became significantly more liberal and on the verge of pacifism. If I can do something to prevent, to make sure no one else has to go off to war, I would. Before that [deployment] a lot of people have a romanticized version of what war would be like, of the camaraderie, and things like that. It took me living through that to realize you don't go to war for the camaraderie, *the camaraderie is what gets you through that experience.* I was never like that before.

Participant B: War changed my moral stance. Over the course of my combat experience, I went from being a Christian, to an agnostic, to an avowed atheist.

In both of these cases, participants admit to enormous shifts and/or loss of belief systems as a direct result of their experience in war. Participant A reluctantly admits that his experience changed his political beliefs drastically. Participant B has suffered a complete crisis of faith and doesn't simply doubt the existence of God, but his experience has convinced him that God actively *does not* exist. While each of these veterans may feel guilt and shame at what they have done or failed to do, it is clear that something else is going on here. In other cases, the structures of the world crumble as they speak.

Participant C: You go out and build these missions to go out and talk to bad people and then soldiers die. . . . It's nothing that you meant to happen, but the fact that they still would be here if you had not said "go find this person" or "go to this location." So, you have that. And you sort of learn to put it into perspective, I guess. *You try to put it into perspective. You try to think of the greater good that you caused some harm, some loss of life, but it balances out by the greater good. But there's no guarantee that that happens. [laughs, long pause] It doesn't happen.*

Here we can hear the veteran continue to struggle to place the events of war within a moral system of where things fit neatly into boxes labeled "right" and "wrong." It is clear that on some level, she believes that she is on the "good side," that she was sent to foster the greater good. We can hear her struggling to find the balance. The story that she is telling herself is this: If bad things happen there must be a greater good that they aim for. But then the participant immediately admits that there is no guarantee of that. The incredible responsibility that the veteran carried meant that lives were lost at *her* orders. They were in some very real sense *her* fault. But this isn't the only thing that the veteran here is struggling with. It's also that there is no way to reconcile the experience *in general.* It's not just that she has done something wrong (which, arguably, she *hasn't*) and is haunted by that, but also that when she tries to use her old moral structures to make sense of it by explaining that lives were lost but that ultimately there was a greater good, she realizes that the structures she previously believed in *no longer hold.*

Finally, one of the participants struggles explicitly with the realization that combat changed him. His experience at war showed him that he is fully capable of killing and what he is surprised and troubled by is his *lack* of shame or guilt. In the passage below, he describes a pivotal moment on deployment.

Participant F: Where we deployed in Iraq, one of their biggest tactics was, um, they used female suicide bombers. So there was a school there for special needs girls, and they would take the girls, anywhere from 10–15 years old, and they would take them out of the school and rig those explosives and tell them to walk. . . . That changed my moral compass. . . . I have no problem shooting guys in the face. You know, it's like, ahh, that's the reason . . . I mean, that, just really, I mean that was something for me, that I was like [I realized] I do not have any issues, that I can sleep real good at night knowing I shot these guys in the face. . . . That's tough.

What is "tough" for this soldier is not just the knowledge that young, special-needs girls are being used as suicide bombers (undeniably a tough thing to witness and realize), but also *what the experience of that did to his beliefs*. Namely, it gave him a perfectly justifiable reason to kill. And not just to kill, but to "[shoot] these guys in the face" and "sleep real good at night knowing" that.

There is a contradiction here that the veteran cannot unravel. He knows that he is not a monster, and yet, he feels no guilt at what he has done (something he would have previously taken as monstrous). This does not square with his previously held beliefs about the moral structure of the world. He is, in some important sense, not the same person before he deployed; he does not have the same moral views; and he does not see the world the same anymore. Before deployment, he lived in a world where killers were troubled by their deeds; after deployment, he is a killer and untroubled by his actions. What is "tough" for him is *not* the action; it is the realization that he is *not* troubled by his actions.

These five accounts are incredibly varied. In the first, the veteran struggles with survivor guilt and the structures of good and evil. In the second and third, veterans experience drastic shifts of moral belief systems, one shift is political and the other religious. In the fourth, we see a veteran actively try and reconcile her guilt with some larger meaning and then fail because she realizes that those structures of meaning are no longer there. In the fifth, we see a veteran disturbed by his lack of guilt, struggling to understand why he isn't a monster if he has acted like one. What links these varied accounts together is the universal experience that war has *fundamentally altered their world view*—how their experience has stamped their horizon and changed how they perceive the world and who they are within it. Each of these individuals is indeed haunted, not simply by what they have done or failed to do, but by the fact that their particular experience in war has changed their world.

What the phenomenological approach allows, then, is a vantage point of the traumatic injury that reveals the way that the event can reverberate through the entire phenomenal field and drastically change the way that the subject experiences herself within that world. This lens is not merely additive—without it we do not have the whole story. Again, this comes to bear on treatment. Think of Shay's veteran who not only feels survivor guilt for being the one spared while his fellow soldier died but also struggles with the senseless nature of the way that he died. It may be possible for him to find a way to forgive himself for his own surviving, but what about the senselessness? Current treatment methods do not account for that part of the injury. What about the third participant, who no longer believes that God exists? Or the fourth who has just realized, mid-interview, that there is no greater good? These ghosts—because they are unrecognized—don't get shaken off. They hold on, continue haunting, interrupting, being a burden, and over the years, they get much heavier.

BANISHING GHOSTS: CREATING A RELATIONAL HOME

If there is a different ghost—if veterans are haunted by what their experience reveals about the world as well as the specific experiences themselves—how can we move toward addressing this? How can we begin to banish *these* ghosts? In a certain way, this question is impossible to answer here. If what we are haunted by—what we bring in—is as varied as we are, there is no neat and singular answer.

I want to conclude by suggesting that there is a general answer to be found in learning how to build better relational homes. For this, I will turn back to Robert Stolorow. Stolorow is a psychoanalyst and philosopher who specializes in the phenomenology of trauma. His is the book that Russell Carr brought to Iraq with him to create short-term treatment plans for soldiers experiencing combat stress on deployment. Before examining his idea of relational homes, it is worth looking briefly at the way his definition of trauma differs from the typical clinical conception.

Stolorow argues that the main feature of traumatic experience is that it is emotionally unbearable, and it lies outside of relational experience. In his words, trauma is *overwhelming affect that lacks a relational home*.[9] Notice that the specific contours of the traumatic event are basically irrelevant here—for something to be traumatic, it simply needs to be experienced as traumatic. In this way, the definition is solidly grounded in the phenomenological stance. The underlying assumption of this half of the equation is that an event (any event) that causes one to feel unbearable emotion can become a traumatic event. It is important to note that this definition places the authority back into the hands of the victim (rather than it being up to the world of clinical psychology to decide what counts as a traumatic event and what does not).

While stripping the definition from specific types of traumatic stressors may seem to make the definition too wide, the word "unbearable" prevents the definition from becoming trivial. Unbearable—literally that which cannot be endured—still sets the bar for traumatic experience quite high. Though we may see the language of trauma littered through our lives in exaggerated ways "That math test was traumatizing!" or "The movers didn't come on the right day and it was traumatic!" here the word serves as a substitute for annoying, frustrating, upsetting. None of these experiences would qualify as unbearable.

The unbearability of trauma can be seen in the initial reaction to the traumatic event, and it is also entangled in the symptoms of PTSD. We shut our eyes in the face of that which we cannot bear, we try and push it away, ignore it, or escape from it. In these frantic attempts, our hearts race, we become hyperfocused, or we dissociate. And yet, as we have seen no matter how hard we try, *that which we cannot bear remains present*—waiting to be carried, demanding to be borne—it haunts us, manifests in symptoms, alters our experience of the world, appears unbidden in our dreams and memories, and blocks us off from the present moment. Trauma hovers, waiting for us, unrelenting.

This is only one half of the definition though—the other necessary condition for an experience to be traumatic, as Stolorow specifies, "lack of relational home."[10] Stolorow holds (and this seems relatively uncontroversial) that our selves are fundamentally relational. In other words, a core part of the self is given over to and embedded within the social structures we are surrounded by. We are influenced by our family of origin, by the society that we grow up in, in the relationships we choose, and so on. We are partially constituted by and through our relationships with other people. Given our social embeddedness and our shared experiential horizon (as Merleau-Ponty might term it), most of what we experience in our lives is relatable. To relate means "to connect," but it also means "to tell." When we relate experiences to others, we narrate with the goal of connecting with others in that telling.

For most of our lives, there are social narratives that are available that match what we are experiencing, or we can at least find a group of people who can intimately understand what we have just gone through. Most of the funny, embarrassing, touching, and sometimes even the tragic experiences that we have are experiences that we can find relational homes for. A relational home is provided when we find a person (or group of people) who can *resonate* with our experience, who can sit with us as we live through or remember our experience, and *relate* to us in it. If our stories are like things we carry, relational homes are psychic places where we can lay those things down and find other people to help us understand them, organize them, and carry them. This relational part of human experience is critical in a number of ways. It helps us to categorize, understand, and process our lives. It connects us with others, helps us feel understood in the experiences that threaten to isolate us, and this connection facilitates trusting relationships.

Relational homes are not simply neutral places where we can rest our burdens, they are dynamic and bivalent. We share our stories with one another so that we can heal and also so that others can resonate and heal as well. We can see the power of this kind of relating when we think of the impact that mental illness memoirs have on those in the midst of their suffering. William Styron, who struggled with alcoholism and depression, wrote the stunning memoir Darkness Visible, which first appeared in *Vanity Fair* in 1989 and then later was published as a stand-alone memoir. His daughter Alexandra (who has since written a memoir of her own) wrote about how people would stop her in the street with tears in their eyes and say, "My god, are you Bill Styron's daughter? You have no idea how [Darkness Visible] changed my life!"[11] This is what Stolorow means by a relational home—in his relating, his telling, Styron provided (and still provides even posthumously) a place for people to come and lay their burdens down, to feel less alone, more validated, and see that there is hope even in the darkest nights of the soul.

As we saw in chapter 3, in order for someone to move beyond the traumatic ground zero of unbearable pain, she must successfully adapt to it, and, in keeping with Stolorow's definition, that means locating a relationship in which she can resonate with someone else in the trauma, where she can gradually feel through and process (or endure that which she could not at the time). So, in the barest terms, a relational home is simply an intersubjective space where another person can help the individual bear those emotions and successfully put the event into the past. As he observes, "Painful emotional experiences become enduringly traumatic in the absence of an intersubjective context within which they can be held and integrated."[12]

So, what constitutes relating in this way? What are the necessary conditions for a relational home? There are three things that I want to gesture at here that can help us understand how to bear witness to those who are traumatized: empathy, attunement, and resonance.

Fundamentally, relating seems to be about empathy—a feeling that is notoriously hard to define and understand. At its core, empathy means to understand—*to perceive the meaning of*—something. Though the core of this definition suggests that what we resonate with is the feeling (rather than the content) of the experience, we make the mistake of thinking that we cannot empathize with that which we have not directly experienced. This becomes a major barrier in the case of veterans, as they constitute such a small percentage of our population and thus come home to a society that is completely unfamiliar with the intricacies of their overwhelm. However, it need not be the case that we share in the experience of combat if we can resonate with the feelings of the overwhelm in general. In Leslie Jamison's book *The Empathy Exams*, she defines empathy in the following way.

> Empathy comes from the Greek empatheia—em (into) and pathos (feeling)—a penetration, a kind of travel. It suggests you enter another person's pain as you'd enter another country, through immigration and customs, border crossing by way of query: What grows where you are? What are the laws? What animals graze there?[13]

Notice that this travel involves a curiosity, a being with, a *becoming familiar* with someone else's pain. Curiosity flies in the face of stereotyping—the root of curiosity is an assumption that one *does not know*, and also that one is open to learning. This learning happens from a position of openness. Notice also that when empathy is defined this way, it does not involve already being familiar with the experience. We have a misconception that in order to help relate with someone that we need to have been through the exact same thing. The travel that Jamison mentions here involves becoming familiar with someone's pain in a way that does not necessarily involve already having experienced it. Jamison instead emphasizes the willingness to be curious, to ask questions with the goal of becoming familiar with what it is like. It is possible to become familiar while being with someone in their foreign world of trauma.

When Carr used Stolorow's phenomenological approach to inform his own treatment of soldiers, what he changed was the way he witnessed the accounts of his patients. In feeling through the experience with them, Carr was able to provide a space in which the trauma could be relived. Instead of just getting the patient to relive the experience as it occurred until the memory became desensitized, Carr joined the patient in their isolating and overwhelming experience and resonated with them in it. In this experience, the unbearable emotion becomes bearable as it finds a relational home in the empathetic reaction of the therapist.

We can see here that there is more going on than just feeling with or feeling alongside. The words "bearing the pain together" suggest something much deeper. Carr is *resonating* with the stories of his patients, he is in attunement with them. Resonance, understood through the lens of physics, is when a sound wave gets reflected from a surface and gains from that reflection (meaning it gets reinforced or prolonged). The reflective surface can be still and silent or it can be vibrating too. When there is vibration from both objects, reinforcing and prolonging the wave, this is attunement. Here the sound is reflected by a synchronous vibration, rather than mirrored back by an object. Two sounds are brought together in harmony.

In phenomenology, resonation is what *underlies* perception and reveals our place in the world. As Merleau-Ponty says,

> We are not this pebble, but when we look at it, it *awakens resonances* in our perceptive apparatus; our perception appears to come from it. That is to say our perception of the pebble is a kind of promotion to (conscious) existence for itself; it is our recovery of this mute thing which, from the time it enters our life, begins to unfold its implicit being, which is revealed to itself through us. What we believe to be coincidence is coexistence.[14]

Our perception—which appears to come from the outside—is actually the inside reflecting the outside back out. It is in this resonance that the space is created where things can "unfold their being" and be revealed to us. We don't see the objects passively, we *coexist* with them.

To bring this all together, what we are doing when we create a relational home is resonating with, reflecting back, vibrating synchronously. As we saw in chapter 4, this allows the victim of trauma to co-create a narrative with someone who can restore the inner dyad. It also lessens the burden of the emotional trauma. Because of this resonance, this attunement provides a way for the sound, the story, the emotional weight to be shared. The patient experiences another person feeling their feelings at the same time, and so it enables them to lift themselves out of isolation. The trauma becomes enveloped in the attunement, and the victim shares it (and all that comes with it) with someone else.[15]

In other words, the traumatic event, when partially borne by another individual, can stop being so isolating and pathological. It can gradually be named, understood, and placed in the past so that the symptoms slowly diminish. When successful, this helps integrate the emotional experience of trauma. This does not mean that the trauma goes away, just that the traumatic experience gets re-ordered so that it stops monopolizing the present. The phenomenological perspective provided by Stolorow allowed Carr to access his patients from the inside. The phenomenological lens draws our attention to the importance of the victim's lived experience of the recent trauma and the ways in which that experience had altered their beliefs about and experience within the world. This enabled Carr to go with the patient into the past experience and relate to the patient in that moment, that is to feel and bear some of that emotion with them, creating a relational home for their overwhelming emotional experience. Juxtapose this with Morris's experience in PE. He says specifically that though there was someone else in the room, he felt that *he was going into the past alone*.

So to create a relational home, what is required is that you simply meet the trauma victim in the overwhelm. This does not require that you already understand it, but that you are willing to approach it with curiosity. It is likely that even in the most foreign of experiences, it is possible to find one core thread of the story that you can resonate with. One may not have been in combat but may understand what it is like to feel terrified for one's life or to feel alienation, or disappointment, or traumatic loss. If it is true that a part of what is so disorienting about trauma is that one loses one's blueprint for the world, it is *this* loss, *this* burden, *this* ghost (the ghost of the world of no meaning) that must be resonated with and laid to rest. This is less about the specific experience of combat and much more about what those experiences *mean*. When we draw our attention away from the specific, singular traumatic event, and toward the global experience of trauma, it becomes more possible to relate to one another.

Veterans often talk about this relational home inadvertently, using the language of "getting it." What is most important is that the listener "gets it," it being the core of the experience, not the specific content. While interviewing veterans, this idea came up repeatedly (to the surprise of myself and sometimes also to the surprise of the veteran). One individual shared that the person in their life that they feel like "gets it" the most is someone who was not a combat veteran and, in fact, is not someone that they have much in common with personally or politically. However, this person spent time in the Peace Corps in West Africa. The interviewee said that he felt that unlike anyone else in his life, this person understood, "what it is like to do a tough thing in a crazy spot." Here we see that it is the core of the experience is what matters, not the specific content. It is worth mentioning that this veteran has a job in which they are surrounded by other veterans, so he's theoretically among many people who should theoretically "get it" if getting it means "experiencing the same thing."

Another veteran explained that they had one particular family member who would say, "I don't know combat, but I do know loss" or "I don't know combat, but I do know scared." He felt that her simultaneous acknowledgment that she did not know what it was like to be on deployment, but that she did see some threads of experience that she did recognize made it possible for her to resonate with his experience in the right way. He felt that unlike so many other people, who assume they understand what combat is like because they have seen it in the movies, she was willing to hear his experience and connect with him while also being aware that their experiences were not the same. This is so helpful because when you tell someone your story and they understand, the world feels less lonely, the trauma feels less isolating. Again, this does not necessarily mean that the other person has to have been a combat veteran, but that the person needs to be able to resonate with a piece of the core experience.

So how do we banish the ghosts? The answer is that just as there are many ways one can be overwhelmed and traumatized, there are many ways to listen and provide support. What is clear at this point is that *without* an open and empathetic support system—without a relational home—veterans aren't able to really come home at all.

NOTES

1. Primo Levi, *The Reawakening* (New York: Touchstone, 1965), 207–208.
2. William Styron, *Darkness Visible: A Memoir of Madness* (New York: First Vintage Books, 1992), 33.
3. Oliver Sacks, *A Leg to Stand On* (New York: Touchstone, 1984), 5–6.
4. Yealland, *Hysterical Disorders of Warfare*, 3–5.
5. Joe Shoenmann, "Former Nellis AFB Drone Operator On First Kill, PTSD, Being Shunned By Fellow Airmen," *State of Nevada,* Produced by KNPR, January 25, 2015, Podcast, MP3 Audio, 20:17. Accessed August 26, 2018, https://knpr.org/knpr/2015-01/former-nellis-afb-drone-operator-first-kill-ptsd-being-shunned-fellow-airmen.
6. Shay, *Achilles in Vietnam*, 70–71.
7. Nancy Sherman, *Afterwar* (New York: Oxford, 2015), 26.
8. The qualitative data cited here was obtained in compliance with all IRB protocol and has been approved by Institutional Review Boards at both College of the Holy Cross and Old Dominion University.
9. Robert Stolorow, *Trauma and Human Existence: Autobiographical, Psychoanalytic, and Philosophical Reflections* (New York: Routledge, 2015), 10.
10. Stolorow, *Trauma and Human Existence*, 10.
11. Alexandra Styron, interview by Alex Nunes, JSTOR Daily, July 29, 2015. https://daily.jstor.org/feature-william-styron-interview-with-daughter/.
12. Stolorow, *Trauma and Human Existence*, 3 & 10.
13. Leslie Jamison, *The Empathy Exams* (Minneapolis, MN: Graywolf Press, 2014), 6.
14. Maurice Merleau-Ponty, *In Praise of Philosophy and Other Essays*, trans. James M. Edie, John Wild, and John O'Neill (Evanston, IL: Northwestern University Press, 1988), 17.
15. I am deeply indebted to Mark Griffin for explaining resonance from the perspective of physics, but also for helping me see, understand, and live into it.

Epilogue

In this book, I have made three claims about the experience of trauma, specifically combat trauma. The first is that understanding and treating combat trauma requires a dynamic, prismatic approach. It is my contention that as long as trauma research remains limited to any single discipline, our understanding of it will remain incomplete. I have argued that an interdisciplinary model for understanding trauma does not require the denigration of any of the contributing fields, but it does require openness to the consideration of this phenomenon from more than one perspective. It also challenges the belief that trauma can be fully grasped by the sciences alone. The experience of traumatic memory—a central symptom of PTSD—is, I noted, psychologically, neurologically, and phenomenologically distinct from other types of memory. Yet, while parallel, the psychological, neurological, and phenomenological accounts of this memory are by no means identical, let alone equivalent. This distinctness strongly suggests that the experience of trauma (and by extension, that of PTSD) is not limited to one's brain function or one's psychological state. It suggests instead that the experience is a highly complex phenomenon involving distinct but complementary psychological, neurological, and phenomenological dimensions that form a rigorous unity. Accordingly, if we are to understand the experience of trauma fully, we have good reason to adopt an interdisciplinary focus. To return to the issue of nomenclature, it is undeniably necessary and important to examine trauma from the perspective of disease. But we miss out on a full understanding of it when we assume that it is *only* a disease and not also a sickness and not also an illness.

The second claim that I have made here concerns the perspective that is perhaps most overlooked in this connection, at least by scientific investigators, namely, that of phenomenology. Though it is also necessary to consider trauma from the perspectives of psychology and neuroscience, I have argued that it is particularly important to consider it from the perspective of phenomenology. The phenomenological perspective, and specifically that of Merleau-Ponty, allows for three things. First, phenomenology provides a critical stance on reductionist accounts that attempt to reduce the experience of trauma to simple causal explanation. Second, phenomenology allows us to address the phenomenon as it occurs to an embodied being who is engaged dynamically with her environment. Third, phenomenology allows us to return to the holistic, lived experience of trauma. I have argued that Merleau-Ponty approaches the examination of trauma with the goal of seeing it as a lived totality (as much as is possible). We don't simply have an illness, "we live *inside* an illness."[1] In other words, the experience of trauma, which becomes chronic in the case of PTSD, paints the horizon within which the victim exists. This perspective illustrates that a phenomenological approach to trauma (and perhaps any illness) is not merely helpful, but necessary.

The third argument that I have made here is that an interdisciplinary approach to combat trauma that involves psychology, neuroscience, and phenomenology can reframe the way that we understand trauma. The phenomenological approach does not just reflect back into the perspectives of psychology and neuroscience, it also expands them. It is in this expansion that we are able to consider what we may have previously missed—that veterans are haunted by a different kind of ghost altogether.

Each war has its "signature wounds," common injuries usually inflicted by new combat techniques or technologies. These wounds are often problematic precisely because they are not fatal. They are not as merciful as wounds that kill. Instead, they leave behind soldiers who are compromised and tortured. In World War I, mustard gas delivered in artillery shells burned and blistered the flesh of soldiers, caused internal and external bleeding, and stripped the mucous membranes of the bronchial tubes. It rarely killed soldiers, but often left them in excruciating pain for weeks. Petroleum burns from incendiary devices that spread ignited oil across the water were the signature wounds in World War II. Napalm—another petroleum-based weapon that stuck to skin and burned at temperatures upwards of 1,400 degrees Fahrenheit—caused brutal burn wounds in Vietnam. After each of these wars, signature wounds are catalogued and studied, as learning how to manage these wounds and prevent them in the future became a key goal of military researchers. With each war came new technological developments that were designed to improve survival rates of soldiers by preventing these wounds. These developments have been successful, as soldiers in the wars in Iraq and Afghanistan have been able to survive injuries that would have been impossible to survive twenty years ago.

Surviving war comes with its own challenges, as evidenced by the signature wound of the wars in Iraq and Afghanistan, one of which is PTSD. Once again, researchers are attempting to find ways to treat and prevent this signature wound. Since 2007, Congress has appropriated upwards of 1.5 billion dollars to help improve the prevention, diagnosis, and treatment of PTSD.[2] The military has implemented programs for what is called "embedded behavioral health," which relocates teams of behavioral health clinicians out of hospitals and into areas where veterans live to provide more convenient, longer-term support.[3] This embedding also occurs in war zones, as psychologists are placed in remote warfare units to provide screening and early intervention during combat.[4] In locations where clinicians cannot be embedded (or in situations where stigma prevents a soldier from seeing a clinician in person), a related program is used called "telebehavioral health," which refers to the use of videoconferencing therapeutic consultations for combat soldiers.

These interventions are a hopeful sign, and they point to a willingness on behalf of the military to accept PTSD as a legitimate wound, which certainly has not always been the case. The number of veterans with PTSD poses a current crisis that makes understanding and treating PTSD urgent. However, if we restrict the study and treatment of trauma to these particular wars, or exclusively to combat trauma, we run the risk of making the mistake that Kardiner and Herman warn of, creating just another episode in which trauma is studied intensively and then forgotten.

The study of trauma *has been* episodic. But it certainly does not need to remain that way. A critical part of correcting involves understanding why it happens. The study of trauma has been episodic because we forget about trauma in moments of peace. We pick it up again only when there has been a large-scale disaster and enough people are traumatized to warrant the focused study of it.

One of our mistakes is thinking that this forgetting is benign, that it simply means "to fail to remember." Letting those who are traumatized fade from view is *not* benign. It is a kind of negligence and an injustice. To forget those who suffer from trauma is to dehumanize them, to relegate them to a different plane of existence. It is an *annihilating silencing* of those who suffer: a refusal to count their reality as a part of our own.

In her essay, "Philosophical Plumbing"—in which Mary Midgley compares philosophy with, well, plumbing—she writes, "When the concepts that we are living by function badly, they do not usually drip audibly through the ceiling or swamp the kitchen floor. They just quietly distort and obstruct our thinking."[5] It's a haunting idea that conceptual mistakes can be so invisibly insidious and corrosive. When we think about trauma—we need to keep an eye on the history of trauma so that we can see the ways that conceptual mistakes from the past might be infecting our current ideas, and by extension, everything that is touched by those ideas.

A critical part of this book has been to try and understand how the concepts that we are living by are functioning badly. And how might we fix them? To continue the plumbing analogy, we first must find the source of the leak. It is in this spirit that we must think about the history of combat trauma, and where our ideas of trauma in general have their roots. Our current classification of PTSD begins with hysteria—which is a diagnosis that suggests weakness, instability, exaggeration, femininity—how might this impact the way that we understand this phenomenon? How do conceptions of femininity (in a pejorative sense) and weakness get imported from history into clinical and societal understandings of trauma today? Finally, what might happen when we free our understanding of combat trauma from these destructive concepts? We come to see it as it really is: an adaptive response to an overwhelming experience that is rooted in an impulse to survive, a response borne of strength, not weakness.

The *first thing* that trauma was considered to be was a weakness—in particular, a feminine kind of failure to pull oneself together and cope, a gendered kind of madness afflicting only "the fairer sex." Despite the fact that current technological advancements have allowed us to gather more information about the nature of trauma and the biological mechanisms behind the symptoms of PTSD, we have not yet shaken the idea that to be traumatized is to be weak. We may not call trauma "hysteria" anymore, but we still locate it in a dark and shameful place. It is not "manly" to suffer from mental illness or to struggle to cope with fear, panic, and sadness. This does not just impact the way that we see trauma, it also bleeds into the way that we *treat* the traumatized societally and clinically.

The urgency of this issue cannot be understated. Because our badly functioning concepts are quietly distorting our thinking, and meanwhile the blood of our veterans is dripping audibly through the ceiling and swamping the kitchen floor.

NOTES

1. Irwin C. Lieb, "The Image of Man in Medicine," *The Journal of Medicine and Philosophy* 1, no. 2 (1976): 165.
2. United States Government, "Hearing Before the Subcommittee on Military Personnel of the Committee on Armed Services," One Hundred Thirteenth Congress, First Session, April 10, 2013, https://www.gpo.gov/fdsys/pkg/CHRG-113hhrg80753/pdf/CHRG113hhrg80753.pdf.

3. Ibid., 8–9.
4. Ibid., 12.
5. Mary Midgley, "Philosophical Plumbing," *Royal Institute of Philosophy Supplement* 33 (1992): 139.

Bibliography

Abercrombie, E. D., and B. L. Jacobs. "Single-unit Response of Noradrenergic Neurons in the Locus Coeruleus of Freely Moving Cats. II. Adaptation to Chronically Presented Stressful Stimuli." *Journal of Neuroscience* 7 (1987): 2844–2848.

Aho, Kevin. "Medicalizing Mental Health: A Phenomenological Alternative." *Journal of Medical Humanities* 29, no. 4 (2008): 243–259.

Aho, Kevin, and Charles Guignon. "Medicalized Psychiatry and the Talking Cure: A Hermeneutic Intervention." *Human Studies* 34, no. 3 (2011): 293–308.

American Psychiatric Association. *Diagnostic and Statistical Manual of Mental Disorders*, vol. 5. Washington, DC: American Psychiatric Association Press, 2013.

Baker, D. B., S. A. West, W. E. Nicholson, N. N. Ekhator, J. W. Kasckow, K. K. Hill, A. B. Bruce, D. N. Orth, and T. D. Geracioti, Jr. "Serial CSF Corticotropin-releasing Hormone Levels and Adrenocortical Activity in Combat Veterans with Posttraumatic Stress Disorder." *American Journal of Psychiatry* 156 (1999): 585–588.

Besley, A. C. (Tina). "Foucault and the Turn to Narrative Therapy." *British Journal of Guidance and Counselling* 30, no. 2 (2002): 125–143.

Borch-Jacobsen, Mikkel. *Remembering Anna O: A Century of Mystification*. New York: Routledge, 1996.

Bremner, J. Douglas. "Does Stress Damage the Brain? Understanding Trauma-Related Disorders from a Mind-Body Perspective." *Directions in Psychiatry* 24, no. 1 (September 2004): 167–175.

———. "Traumatic Stress: Effects on the Brain." *Dialogs and Clinical Neuroscience* 8 (2006): 445–461.

Bremner, J. D., J. Licinio, A. Darnell, J. H. Krystal, M. J. Owens, S. M. Southwick, C. B. Nemeroff, and D. S. Charney. "Elevated CSF Corticotropin-Releasing Factor Concentrations in Posttraumatic Stress Disorder." *American Journal of Psychiatry* 154 (1997): 624–629.

Bremner, J. Douglas, Penny Randall, Eric Vermetten, Lawrence Staib, Richard A. Bronen, Carolyn Mazure, Sandi Capelli, Gregory McCarthy, Robert B. Innis, and Dennis S. Charney. "MRI-based Measurement of Hippocampal Volume in

Posttraumatic Stress Disorder Related to Childhood Physical and Sexual Abuse: A Preliminary Report." *Biological Psychiatry* 41 (1997): 23–32.

Bremner, J. D., T. M. Scott, R. C. Delaney, S. M. Southwick, J. Mason, and D. Johnson. "Deficits in Short-term Memory in Posttraumatic Stress Disorder." *American Journal of Psychiatry* 150, no. 7 (1993): 1015–1019.

Bremner, J. D., M. Vythilingam, E. Vermetten, J. Adil, S. Khan, A. Nazeer, N. Afzal, T. McGlashan, B. Elzinga, G. M. Anderson, G. Heninger, S. M. Southwick, and D. S. Charney. "Cortisol Response to a Cognitive Stress Challenge in Posttraumatic Stress Disorder (PTSD) Related to Childhood Abuse." *Psychoneuroendocrinology* 28 (2003): 733–750.

Carr, Alan. "Michael White's Narrative Therapy." *Contemporary Family Therapy* 20, no. 4 (1998): 485–503.

Carr, Russell B. "Combat and Human Existence: Toward an Intersubjective Approach to Combat-Related PTSD." *Psychoanalytic Psychology* 28, no. 4 (June 2011): 1–27.

Carroll, D. W. *Psychology of Language, 4th Edition*. Belmont, MA: Wadsworth/Thompson, 2004.

Dahlstrom, Daniel O., Andreas Elpidorou, and Walter Hopp. *Philosophy of Mind and Phenomenology: Conceptual and Empirical Approaches*. New York: Taylor & Francis, 2015.

Damasio, Antonio. *Descartes' Error: Emotion, Reason, and the Human Brain*. New York: Grossett & Putnam, 1994.

Descartes, Rene. *Meditations on First Philosophy*. Translated by John Cottingham. New York: Cambridge University Press, 2013.

Dillon, Max C. *Merleau-Ponty's Ontology*. Bloomington: Indiana University Press, 1988.

Dreyfus, Hubert. "The Current Relevance of Merleau-Ponty's Phenomenology of Embodiment." *Electronic Journal of Analytic Philosophy* 4 (Spring 1996): available at http://ejap.louisiana.edu/EJAP/1996.spring/dreyfus.1996.spring.html.

Elman, J. L., and James L. McClelland. "Cognitive Penetration of the Mechanisms of Perception: Compensation for Co-articulation of Lexically Restored Phonemes." *Journal of Memory & Language* 27 (1988): 143–165.

Felman, Shoshana, and Dori Laub. *Testimony: Crises of Witnessing in Literature, Psychoanalysis, and History*. New York: Routledge, 1991.

Flor, H., T. Elbert, S. Knecht, C. Wienbruch, C. Pantev, N. Birbaumer, W. Larbig, and E. Taub. "Phantom-limb Pain as a Perceptual Correlate of Cortical Reorganization Following Arm Amputation." *Nature* 375, no. 6531 (June 1995): 482–482.

Flor, H., L. Nikolajsen, and T. Jensen Staehilin. "Phantom Limb Pain: A Case of Maladaptive Central Nervous System Plasticity?" *National Review of Neuroscience* 7, no. 11 (November 2006): 873–881.

Foa, Edna, and Terence Keane. *Effective Treatments for PTSD, Second Edition Practice Guidelines from the International Society for Traumatic Stress Studies*. New York: Guilford, 2008.

Foa, Edna, E. A. Hembree, and B. Rothbaum. *Prolonged Exposure Therapy for PTSD: Emotional Processing of Traumatic Experiences: Therapist Guide*. New York: Oxford University Press, 2007.

Freud, Sigmund, and Josef Breuer. *Studies on Hysteria*. Translated by Nicola Luckhurst. London: Penguin, 2004.

Fuchs, Thomas. "Body Memory and the Unconscious." *Phaenomenologica* 199 (2012): 69–82.

Gallagher, Shaun. "On the Possibility of Naturalizing Phenomenology." In *The Oxford Handbook of Contemporary Philosophy*, edited by Dan Zahavi, 70–93. New York: Oxford University Press, 2012, see esp. pp. 82–87.

Gendlin, Eugene. *Experiencing and the Creation of Meaning: A Philosophical and Psychological Approach to the Subjective*. New York: Free Press of Glencoa, 1962.

Goldenberg, Georg. "Goldstein and Gelb's Case Schn: A Classic Case in Neuropsychology?" In *Brain, Behavior and Cognition: Classic Cases in Neuropsychology, Volume II*, edited by Chris Code, Claus-W. Wallesch, Yves Joanette, and Andre Roch Lecours, 281–299. Florence: Psychology Press, 2013.

Goldie, Peter. "One's Remembered Past: Narrative Thinking, Emotion, and the External Perspective." *Philosophical Papers* 32, no. 3 (2003): 301–319.

———. "Narrative Thinking, Emotion, and Planning." *Journal of Aesthetics and Art Criticism* 67, no. 1 (Winter 2009): 97–106.

———. *The Mess Inside: Narrative, Emotion, and the Mind*. New York: Oxford University Press, 2012.

Gurvits, T. V., M. R. Shenton, H. Hokama, H. Ohta, N. B. Lasko, M. W. Gilbertson, S. P. Orr, R. Kikinis, F. A. Jolesz, R. W. McCarley, and R. K. Pitman. "Magnetic Resonance Imaging Study of Hippocampal Volume in Chronic Combat-Related Posttraumatic Stress Disorder." *Biological Psychiatry* 40 (1996): 192–199.

Hass, Lawrence. *Merleau-Ponty's Philosophy*. Bloomington, IN: Indiana University Press, 2008.

Helpman, Liat, Marie-France Marin, Papini Santiago, Xi Zhu, Gregory M. Sullivan, Franklin Schneier, Mariana Neria, Erel Shvil, Maria Josefa Malaga Aragon, John C. Markowitz, Martin Lindquist, Tor Wager, Mohammad Milad, and Yuval Neria. "Neural Changes in Extinction Recall Following Prolonged Exposure Treatment for PTSD: A Longitudinal fMRI Study." *Neuroimage: Clinical* 12 (2016): 715–723.

Herman, Judith. *Trauma and Recovery*. New York: Basic Books, 1999.

Hopper, J. W., P. A. Frewen, B. A. van der Kolk, and R. A. Lanius. "Neural Correlates of Reexperiencing, Avoidance, and Dissociation in PTSD: Symptom Dimensions and Emotion Dysregulation in Responses to Script-Driven Trauma Imagery." *Journal of Traumatic Stress* 20, no. 5 (2007): 713–725.

Hughes, K. C., and L. M. Shin. "Functional Neuroimaging Studies of Post-Traumatic Stress Disorder." *Expert Review of Neurotherapeutics* 11, no. 2 (2011): 275–285.

Hunter, Dianne. "Hysteria, Psychoanalysis, and Feminism: The Case of Anna O." *Feminist Studies* 9, no. 3 (1983): 464–488.

Imperial War Museums Archive. "The Cost of the Common Cold and Influenza." Accessed August 24, 2018. http://www.iwm.org.uk/collections/item/object/31960.

Jamison, Leslie. *The Empathy Exams*. Minneapolis, MN: Graywolf Press, 2014.

Kardiner, Abram. *Traumatic Neuroses of War*. Mansfield, CT: Martino Publishing, 2012.

Kemp, Janet. "Suicide Rates in VHA Patients through 2011 with Comparisons with Other Americans and Other Veterans Through 2010." Veterans Health Administration (2014). Last accessed August 23, 2014. http://www.mentalhealth.va.gov/docs/Suicide_Data_Report_Update_January_2014.pdf.

Kemp, Janet, and Robert Bossarte. "Suicide Data Report, 2012." Department of Veterans Affairs Mental Health Services Suicide Prevention Program (2013). Last accessed November 12, 2014. http://www.va.gov/opa/docs/Suicide-Data-Report-2012-final.pdf.

Knotkova, H., R. A. Cruciani, V. M. Tronnier, and D. Rasche. "Current and Future Options for the Management of Phantom-limb Pain." *Journal of Pain Research* 5 (March 2012): 39–49.

Lanius, R. A., R. L. Bluhm, and P. A. Frewen. "How Understanding the Neurobiology of Complex Post-traumatic Stress Disorder Can Inform Clinical Practice: A Social Cognitive and Affective Neuroscience Approach." *Acta Psychiatrica Scandinavica* (2011): 331–348.

Laub, Dori. "Reestablishing the Internal 'Thou' in Testimony of Trauma." *Psychoanalysis, Culture & Society* 18, no. 2 (2013): 184–198.

———. *Witness*. New Haven, CT: Yale University, 1987. Yale Fortunoff Video Archive. Last accessed on August 29, 2018. http://www.library.yale.edu/testimonies/publications/witness.html.

LeDoux, Joseph. "Emotional Memory Systems in the Brain." *Behavioral Brain Research* 58 (1993): 69–79.

———. *The Emotional Brain: The Mysterious Underpinnings of Emotional Life*. New York: Simon & Schuster, 1996.

———. "Emotion Circuits in the Brain." *Annual Review of Neuroscience* 23 (2000): 155–184.

Levi, Primo. *The Reawakening*. New York: Touchstone, 1965.

Lieb, Irwin C. "The Image of Man in Medicine." *The Journal of Medicine and Philosophy* 1, no. 2 (1976): 162–176.

MacLean, Paul. *The Triune Brain in Evolution: Role in Paleocerebral Function*. New York: Plenum, 1990.

Marotta, J. J., and M. Behrman. "Patient Schn: Has Goldstein and Gelb's Case Withstood the Test of Time?" *Neuropsychologia* 42 (2004): 633–638.

McEwen, Bruce. "Stress, Adaptation, and Disease: Allostasis and Allostatic Load." *Annals of the New York Academy of Sciences* 840 (1998): 33–44.

Merleau-Ponty, Maurice. *Phenomenology of Perception*. Translated by Colin Smith. New York: Routledge, 1962.

———. "Eye and Mind." Translated by Carleton Dallery. In *The Primacy of Perception: And Other Essays on Phenomenological Psychology, the Philosophy of Art, History, and Politics*, edited by James M. Edie, authored by Maurice Merleau-Ponty, 159–190. Evanston, IL: Northwestern University Press, 1964.

———. “The Primacy of Perception and Its Philosophical Consequences.” Translated by James M. Edie. In *The Primacy of Perception: And Other Essays on Phenomenological Psychology, the Philosophy of Art, History, and Politics*, edited by James M. Edie, authored by Maurice Merleau-Ponty, 12–42. Evanston, IL: Northwestern University Press, 1964.

———. *The Structure of Behavior*. Translated by Alden L. Fisher. Pittsburgh: Duquesne University Press, 1983.

———. *In Praise of Philosophy and Other Essays*. Translated by James M. Edie, John Wild, and John O'Neill. Evanston, IL: Northwestern University Press, 1988.

Midgley, Mary. “Philosophical Plumbing.” *Royal Institute of Philosophy Supplement* 33 (1992): 139–151.

Micale, Mark S. “On the ‘Disappearance’ of Hysteria: A Study in the Clinical Deconstruction of a Diagnosis.” *Isis* 84, no. 3 (1993): 496–526.

Morris, David. *The Evil Hours: A Biography of Post-Traumatic Stress Disorder*. New York: Eamon Dolan, 2016.

———. “Trauma Post Trauma.” *Slate Magazine*, July 21st, 2015. Last accessed July 22, 2015. http://www.slate.com/articles/health_and_science/medical_examiner/2015/07/prolonged_exposure_therapy_for_ptsd_the_va_s_treatment_has_dangerous_side.single.html.

Morey, R. A., F. Dolcos, C. M. Petty, D. A. Cooper, J. P. Hayes, K. S. LaBar, and G. McCarthy. “The Role of Trauma Related Distractors on Neural Systems for Working Memory and Emotion Processing.” *Journal of Psychiatric Research* 43, no. 8 (2009): 809–817.

Najavits, Lisa M. “The Problem of Dropout from ‘Gold Standard’ PTSD Therapies.” *F1000 Prime Reports* 7 (2015): 43. https://f1000.com/prime/reports/m/7/43.

Panksepp, Jaak. *Affective Neuroscience*. New York: Oxford University Press, 1998.

Porges, Stephen. “Orienting in a Defensive World: Mammalian Modifications of our Evolutionary Heritage. A Polyvagal Theory.” *Psychophysiology* 32 (1995): 301–318.

Ratcliffe, Matthew. *Real Hallucinations: Psychiatric Illness, Intentionality, and the Interpersonal World.* Cambridge: The MIT Press, 2017.

Richert, Alphons. *Integrating Existential and Narrative Therapy*. Pittsburgh: Duquesne University Press, 2010.

Sacks, Oliver. *A Leg to Stand On*. New York: Touchstone, 1984.

Samuel, A. G. “Phonemic Restoration: Insights from a New Methodology.” *Journal of Experimental Psychology* 110 (1981): 474–494.

Sapolsky, R. M. “Why Stress is Bad for Your Brain.” *Science* 273, no. 5276 (1996): 749–750.

Sapolsky, R. M., H. Uno, C. S. Rebert, and C. E. Finch. “Hippocampal Damage Associated With Prolonged Glucocoricoid Exposure in Primates.” *Journal of Neuroscience* 10 (1990): 2897–2902.

Schmahl, C. G., E. Vermetten, B. M. Elzinga, and J. D. Bremner. “Magnetic Resonance Imaging of Hippocampal and Amygdala Volume in Women with Childhood Abuse and Borderline Personality Disorder.” *Psychiatry Research: Neuroimaging* 122 (2003): 193–198.

Scott, Wilbur. "PTSD in the DSM III, a Case in the Politics of Diagnosis and Disease." *Social Problems* 37, no. 3 (1990): 294–310.

Senecal, Gary, and MaryCatherine McDonald. "Mission Completion, Troop Welfare, and Destructive Idealism." *New Male Studies: An International Journal* 6, no. 2 (2017): 64–89.

Shay, Jonathan. *Achilles in Vietnam: Combat Trauma and the Undoing of Character*. New York: Simon & Schuster, 1995.

Sherman, Nancy. *Afterwar*. New York: Oxford, 2015.

Shin, L. H., R. J. McNally, S. M. Kosslyn, W. L. Thompson, S. L. Rauch, N. M. Alpert, L. J. Metzger, N. B. Lasko, S. P. Orr, and R. K. Pitman. "Regional Cerebral Blood Flow During Script-driven Imagery in Childhood Sexual Abuse-Related PTD: A PET Investigation." *American Journal of Psychiatry* 156 (1999): 575–584.

Shoenmann, Joe. *State of Nevada*. Produced by KNPR. January 25th, 2015. August 26th, 2018. https://knpr.org/knpr/2015-01/former-nellis-afb-drone-operator-first-kill-ptsd-being-shunned-fellow-airmen.

Stolorow, Robert D. *Trauma and Human Existence: Autobiographical, Psychoanalytic, and Philosophical Reflections*. New York: Analytic, 2007.

Stratton, George M. "Some Preliminary Experiments on Vision Without Inversion of the Retinal Image." *Psychological Review* 3, no. 6 (November 1896): 611–617.

———. "Vision Without Inversion of the Retinal Image." *Psychological Review* 4, no. 5 (September 1897): 463–481.

———. "The Spatial Harmony of Touch and Sight." *Mind* 8, no. 32 (October 1899): 492–505.

Styron, Alexandra. JSTOR Daily. By Alex Nunes. July 29th, 2015. https://daily.jstor.org/feature william-styron-interview-with-daughter/.

Styron, William. *Darkness Visible: A Memoir of Madness*. New York: First Vintage Books, 1992.

Tasca, Cecilia, Mariangela Rapetti, Mauro Giovanni Carta, and Bianca Fadda. "Women and Hysteria in the History of Mental Health." *Clinical Practice and Epidemiology in Mental Health* 8, no. 1 (2012): 110–119.

Trudeau, D. L., J. Anderson, L. M. Hansen, D. N. Shaglov, J. Schmoller, S. Nugent, and S. Barton. "Findings of Mild Traumatic Brain Injury in Combat Veterans with PTSD and a History of Blast Concussion." *The Journal of Neuropsychiatry and Clinical Neurosciences* 10, no. 3 (1998): 308–313.

United States Department of Veterans Affairs. "Prolonged Exposure Therapy for PTSD." Accessed August 29, 2018. https://www.ptsd.va.gov/public/treatment/therapy med/prolonged-exposure-therapy.asp.

United States Government. "Hearing Before the Subcommittee on Military Personnel of the Committee on Armed Services." One Hundred Thirteenth Congress, First Session, April 10th, 2013. https://www.gpo.gov/fdsys/pkg/CHRG-113hhrg80753/pdf/CHRG113hhrg80753.pdf

Van der Hart, Onno, and Rutger Horst. "The Dissociation Theory of Pierre Janet." *Journal of Traumatic Stress* 2, no. 4 (1989): 1–11.

Van der Kolk, Bessel A. "Trauma and Memory." *Psychiatry and Clinical Neurosciences* 52 (1998): 52–64.

———. "Posttraumatic Stress Disorder and the Nature of Trauma." *State of the Art: Dialogues in Clinical Neuroscience* 2, no. 1 (2000): 7–22.

———. "Clinical Implications of Neuroscience Research in PTSD." *Annals of the New York Academy of Sciences* 1071 (2006): 277–293.

———. *The Body Keeps the Score: Brain, Mind, and Body in the Healing of Trauma.* New York: Viking Penguin, 2014.

Van Der Kolk, Bessel A., Alexander C. McFarlane, and Lars Weisæth. *Traumatic Stress: The Effects of Overwhelming Experience on Mind, Body, and Society*. New York: Guilford, 1996.

Van Der Kolk, Bessel A., and Lisa M. Najavits. "Interview: What is PTSD Really? Surprises, Twists of History, and the Politics of Diagnosis and Treatment." *Journal of Clinical Psychology: In Session* 69, no. 5 (2013): 516–522.

Veith, Ilza. *Hysteria: The History of a Disease*. Chicago: University of Chicago Press, 1965.

Warren, R. M. "Perceptual Restoration of Missing Speech Sounds." *Science* 167, no. 3917 (1970): 392–393.

———. "Auditory Illusions and Confusions." *Scientific American* 223 (December 1970): 30–36.

White, Michael, and David Epston. *Narrative Means to Therapeutic Ends.* New York: W.W. Norton & Company, 1990.

Yealland, Lewis. *Hysterical Disorders of Warfare*. London: Macmillan, 1918.

Index

About the Author

Dr. MaryCatherine McDonald is assistant professor of philosophy at Old Dominion University. Her research lies at the junctures of philosophy, psychology, and neuroscience. She is particularly interested in the lived experience of trauma and mental illness, as well as looking critically at diagnostic frameworks and the way that technology is deployed in psychological research.

www.ingramcontent.com/pod-product-compliance
Lightning Source LLC
Chambersburg PA
CBHW031414220926
51612CB00004B/6
9781498580427